LAST OF THE
MOE HAIRCUTS

LAST OF THE MOE HAIRCUTS

BILL FLANAGAN

CONTEMPORARY
BOOKS, INC.
CHICAGO • NEW YORK

Library of Congress Cataloging-in-Publication Data

Flanagan, Bill.
    Last of the Moe haircuts.

    1. Three Stooges films—Anecdotes, facetiae, satire,
etc.   2. Three Stooges (Comedy team)—Anecdotes,
facetiae, satire, etc.   I. Title.
PN1995.9.T5F58   1986   791.43′028′0922   86-6263
ISBN 0-8092-5152-3 (pbk.)

"The Influence of the Three Stooges on Rock 'n' Roll"
first appeared in *Musician* magazine. Another
version of "The Effects of the Three Stooges on the
Ayatollah Khomeini" has appeared in *Rhode Island Review*.

Published by Contemporary Books, Inc.
180 North Michigan Avenue, Chicago, Illinois 60601
Manufactured in the United States of America
International Standard Book Number: 0-8092-5152-3

Published simultaneously in Canada by Beaverbooks, Ltd.
195 Allstate Parkway, Valleywood Business Park
Markham, Ontario L3R 4T8 Canada

Contents

To the Nahods

Introduction

MENTION THE FRENCH Reign of Terror to any schoolchild, and the child will think of Robespierre. Ask who dominated Britain in the last days of the nineteenth century, and even an idiot will burble, "Queen Victoria." Yet while any moron knows that the Three Stooges have dominated the twentieth century's culture, moral direction, and political thought, it seems as if those morons are the *only* ones who know.

How is it that lesser influences like Leon Trotsky, Albert Schweitzer, and Carl Yastrzemski have received so much credit, while Moe, Larry, and Curly (in whose place Shemp was called) are rarely mentioned in academic texts? Why are Howard, Fine, and Howard the subject of fewer doctoral dissertations than Herman Hesse?

There has been a conspiracy of ignorance against the Stooges, a conspiracy against admitting the obvious debt our entire culture owes to the Stooges. It is a conspiracy this slender volume will begin to expose. But first, we must take a look at the Great Art of the Stooges, for in denying the Stooges their status as Great Art, shortsighted critics and historians have denied Howard, Fine, and Howard acknowledgment of the enormous influence their art has inspired.

How do I know the Stooges are Great Art? Well, if the only standard I had to meet to make such an assertion were that of

Curly, Larry, and . . . Mao.

the populist, it would be acceptable just because I said so. But I do not set the Stooges' sights so low. Rather, Moe, Larry, and Curly meet the only standard for judging great art that is inarguable and against which all protests fade: they withstand the test of time. No one can finally maintain Euripedes didn't have the right stuff, because Euripedes' plays speak to audiences across generations in a way that the works of many of his peers do not. Beethoven may have been controversial during his lifetime, but the continued success of his music with disparate audiences makes moot the arguments of his detractors. Art, civilization agrees, is finally proven by its ability to speak to new audiences in strange tongues long after its makers have stopped drawing breath or residuals.

Who, then, in the twentieth century, can lay claim to more artistic legitimacy than the Three Stooges? Who else has spoken with equal ease to peoples as diverse as the migrants and apple peddlers of the Great Depression, the hula-hooped babies of the "Howdy Doody" era, and the punks, priests, and physicians of the 1980s? College students regard Chaplin as an academic assignment as dusty as *She Stoops to Conquer,* but Curly and his partners reduce them to the same hysterics they did their grandparents. Is that typical of slapstick or vulgar art? Not at all—no other comedy (or radio show or comic book) of the Stooges' era gets a comparable reaction. No, to find contemporaries of the Three Stooges whose impact on succeeding generations is commensurate, we must look to Picasso, to Hemingway, to Einstein. These men can make claim to being peers of Howard, Fine, and Howard, though one wonders if any of them could say as much with their strokes, prose, or physics as Moe could with one well-aimed pie.

Detractors continue to die horrible deaths, while the antics of Curly, Larry, and Moe win the hearts of generation after generation. Theirs is the only true immortality. When the great empires of our time are no more, when the names of today's celebrities are forgotten, when our customs are antique and our innovations quaint, there will still be a blue light emanating from some distant satellite and an electronic voice intoning, "Nyuk nyuk nyuk." That, dear readers, is the Last Laugh.

Bill Flanagan
American Stooge Symposium
October 1985

It was impossible for preeminent thinkers of the 20th century to escape the influence of the Stooges. Freud acknowledged his debt by commissioning this poignant self-portrait, where he literally stands in the shadow of his models for the ego (Larry), the superego (Moe), and the id (who else?). What's Bertrand Russell doing there? Only Siggy knows for sure.

About the American Stooge Symposium

THIS TEXT GREW out of my work with the ASS, an august educational institution that roams the American cultural wasteland, lecturing on the social and artistic contributions of Howard, Fine, and Howard. *Last of the Moe Haircuts* would not have been realized without the input of my distinguished colleagues, the three principle professors of the ASS:

James E. Kelleher, parochial school educator, Irish tenor, student of jurisprudence and political science. Kelleher named this book and might well have won its dedication had he not already been so honored by the author of *Daniel and Drum Rock*.

Rudy Cheeks, newspaper columnist, radio talk show host, film scholar, cable TV star, moviemaker, jazz soloist. Cheeks took my concept of Stooge seminars and made them a reality. He rented the films, secured the halls, organized the presentations, chaired the panels, and pocketed the profits.

Jeff Shore, archaeologist, paleontologist, restaurateur, ivory tickler, man of independent means. Shore's knowledge of the arcane alleys of Stoogedom made him the Symposium's living encyclopedia and reference file. It was Shore who bought the pies.

Very special thanks to Janet Watt, who provided the fine art illustrations for this volume and who, with Gene, gave our symposium its first home, at Providence's late, lamented One Up. That this once noble hall of learning has been converted into a Yuppie pickup parlor says a great deal about our society's sad priorities.

Stephen Braks provided hours of Stooge videos; Lou Papineau and Tony Lioce came up with some rare photos; Gail Kelleher developed the theory of Moe-Town; Wind was performing "Curly, Larry & Moe" ten years before the "Curly Shuffle."

Finally, a back-wrenching bow to Michael Nahod, naval officer, botanist, linguist, Japanese resident, flautist, and Doctor of Stoogeology. Compiling detailed lists of Moe's threats and epithets is the least of Nahod's Stoogely accomplishments. Before entering the navy in 1978, Nahod compiled an astonishing personal library of Stooge's films and memorabilia. He played tape recordings of Stooge's soundtracks as others play records. It was Nahod's evangelical zest that opened many young minds to the deeper levels of Moeist thought. As long as the U.S. military boasts leaders of Nahod's caliber, our defense budget is well spent, our shores secure.

Correspondence to the American Stooge Symposium may be sent care of the *Newpaper*, Suite 209, 131 Washington St., Providence, RI 02903. There is no guarantee that we will open, read, or answer any mail. We just like annoying the *Newpaper*.

1

The Influence of the Three Stooges on Rock 'n' Roll

IT HAS BEEN said that all rock 'n' roll since the mid-sixties has been a variation on either Bob Dylan, the Beatles, or the Rolling Stones. That this is true does not preclude an even earlier universal antecedent: *all* rock music can finally be traced to either Moe, Larry, or Curly.

The Three Stooges, before Elvis or Little Richard, before Brando or James Dean, blasted apart the consciousness of the postwar generation and reassembled it in their own image. As quickly as the pure product of Howard, Fine, and Howard was picked up by television, kids across America went crazy. Parents reacted with a horror typical of (but by no means restricted to) the McCarthy era. Mothers campaigned to have the Stooges banned, and dozens of TV stations knuckled under. PTAs condemned their "harmful, morally debased" influence. The reaction of fifties middle America to the early rockers was tame compared to the panic the Stooges excited.

Rock 'n' roll only reflected the cultural hegemony of Moe, Larry, and Curly. If the new music was mothered by country and the blues, it was fathered by the Three Stooges in a riotous gang-bang of post-Hiroshima rebellion. "We want the world and we want it *now*," a generation screamed—but it was a child's tentative imitation of Moe Howard's ambitious, all-purpose "Who do we have to kill?"

But if the Stooges provided the soul and inspiration, can

rock at least take credit for coming up with the melody? Certainly not. The Stooges themselves were often portrayed playing musical instruments (with somewhat more technical dexterity than, say, Presley or Dylan), singing in close harmony (the Beach Boys and the Four Seasons appropriated many of their high, some would say shrill, vocal arrangements from Curly and the boys), and improvising lyrics that defied the accepted moon/June banalities of the day. Yet, if their influence on music was all-pervasive, if their antiauthoritarian politics were finally globe-shaking, it was the Stooges' haircuts that truly revolutionized the Aquarian generation.

Moe was, of course, the leader, the asserter, the oldest brother, and for a time the flower of rock—the leaders and asserters—all appropriated Moe Hair. When the Beatles copied Moe's pudding bowl coiffure to the finest detail, the civilized world followed suit.

Just as the leaders followed Moe, the passive, docile, and sensitive emulated Larry Fine's locks. Art Garfunkel was most prominent among the sons of Larry. Like Larry, Garfunkel had a Moe-Haired Paul Simon threatening him, pushing him around, and generally leaving him "low man again."

Noel Redding and Mitch Mitchell of the Jimi Hendrix Experience were forced to play *dual* Larrys—posing on the cover of *Electric Ladyland* in a loving re-creation of the portrait that introduced the Stooges' earliest shorts.

Curly's followers were, like himself, misfits, morons, and geeks. Ian Dury capitalized on being slightly crippled (as Curly was) and shaved his head to affect a Curly-do. Later, the most despairing and nihilistic of Britain's punks—the skinheads and Oi Boys—continued the cult.

Lyrically, the Stooges had the most obvious influence on Steely Dan, whose songs often seemed stylized, jazzed-up variations on Stooge tunes. "Swing it!" cried Curly to the band again and again, his prototypical prebop hipster the model for Steely Dan's Deacon Blue. It takes little imagination to picture Curly loose in a hospital, wheeling a gurney down a corridor and warbling, "Is there gas in the car? Yes, there's gas in the car."

Bob Dylan cried out in "Highway 61," the title song of his

 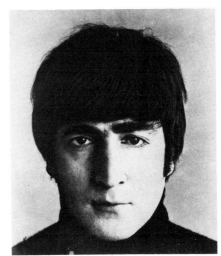

Moe, John: The leaders, the asserters, Moe Haircuts.

greatest album, "I asked Moe Howard, 'Where can I go?' " The rock world was following Dylan's direction, but Dylan was following the Stooges.

At the height of his concerts, Bruce Springsteen has been known to fall on his side and run in circles on the floor in the manner of Curly throwing a fit. NRBQ recorded a song called "Doctor Howard, Doctor Fine, Doctor Howard," and the Del-Lords took their name from the great Stooge director Del Lord.

When Joe Strummer and others of rock's last generation finally found a haircut not worn by a Stooge, they named it in tribute to them: they called it a Moe-Hawk.

No rock act, however, approached the elegant simplicity of the Stooges' great "Swingin' the Alphabet" ("B-I-Bee, B-O-Bo, B-I-Bickey Bi") until the Police copped the formula with "De Do Do Do, De Da Da Da" in 1980. To promote the album containing that song, the bleached blonde popsters released a video that showed them dancing at a classroom chalkboard in robes and mortarboards, an obvious visual reference to the same seminal Stooges short.

Yet of all the rockers who found their own philosophy in the Stooges' vision, none re-created their personas so perfectly in concert with that spiritual city of light we call Moe-Town as

Buster Bloodvessel of new wave band Bad Manners. Photo by Bob Elsdale.

did Crosby, Stills, and Nash. These three folkies virtually dedicated their lives to becoming Stooges incarnate. In the end they succeeded far more gloriously than Joes Besser and DeRita ever did.

From his lovey-dovey "We're all brothers" beginnings, Stephen Stills evolved a full Moe persona. He became angry, belligerent, and downright rude. Stills would perform in huge hockey rinks and then chew out the audience if anyone talked during one of his songs. Insiders are sure Stephen once told a lackey, "Remind me to kill you later."

Neil Young, sheepdoggish with his shaggy black hair parted in the middle, was Shemp to Stills's Moe. Shemp and Moe had been partners before the Stooges, like Stills and Young before CSN, and when there was a chance, the old buddy was brought into the new act. Still, both long relationships periodically exploded into conflict, and both ended with Moe/Stills continuing the trio without Shemp/Young.

Graham Nash, wimpy and equivocating, was the finest Fine since Larry himself.

That left it to David Crosby to achieve the most difficult "transmorgification" of all—to go from a talented and articulate singer/songwriter to an overweight, shiny-headed pratfaller. Curly's own hobbled gait was the result of having once shot himself in the foot, and if Crosby never duplicated that stunt literally, he pulled it off figuratively a dozen times. It is perhaps the greatest tribute to his Stoogely influences that, when we think of Crosby in years to come, our image of him will surely be of a rotund maniac, madly fleeing a pursuing gaggle of police, those once lovely harmonies now a trilling, fading, "Woo woo woo woo woo."

2

The Effect of the Stooges on Literature

I WOULD NOT WANT to say Jack Kerouac and I were close friends. This is no put-down of Jack. Sure, we both came from New England, got into the Beat scene in New York's Greenwich village, did some serious cross-country driving, and then made our marks as hip authors for the young generation. But for all that, I wouldn't want to call Jack Kerouac a close friend, for he died when I was in the ninth grade, and I never laid eyes on the guy. I just want to clear this up in case some future E. L. Doctorow decides to do a historical novel that makes Kerouac and me neighbors on Bleeker Street or something. All I know of the joker is that he appealed to the girls in English class who wrote long confessional poems without capital letters.

I once believed that Kerouac had a lot to do with inventing the Beat's stream-of-consciousness, jazz-influenced writing style. That was before I looked back a generation to the jazz-tinged cadences of the Three Stooges. Listen to Curly's monologue from *Disorder in the Court* and then tell me Kerouac, Ginsberg, and Burroughs were innovators:

"Me and my pals, we're musicians. We were tearin' up some hot swing music in the orchestra; Gail over there was swinging her fans. Her sweetie Kirk Robin was inhaling a

bottle of hootch at a table, and a hoofer by the name of Buck
Wing was getting ready to shake his tootsies."

There's more, but you get the drift. The Stooges took Hemingway's then-fresh chop-chop style and imbued its cadence
with street-smart slang. This was, in itself, enough to keep
Dashiell Hammett and Raymond Chandler going for years. But
the jazz imagery and rhythms Curly employed had an elastic-
ity Hemingway and his hard-boiled acolytes couldn't accomplish within their clipped meter. In Curly's use, the spice of
the swear word also had the wings of song (probably "Bread in
Old Kentucky"). Most of what the Beats did a generation later
was nothing more than a rehash of the Stooges' literary
innovations.

Some wise-ass critics have claimed that Moe and the boys
copped their licks from the cats who wrote their scripts. What
a hunk of baloney! That's like saying Coltrane doing "Favorite
Things" was a rehash of "The Sound of Music"! Sure, the
Stooges usually based their improvs, their flights of imagination, on the work of credited screenwriters. You want to make
something out of that? Take it up with William Shakespeare
who based his own plays on earlier plots. But for the record,
the writing credit on 1934's *Punch Drunks* is given to Jerry
Howard, Larry Fine, and Moe Howard. The extra dedication
the Stooges put into this particular script is evidenced by the
fact that all the characters in it talk like Moe. (When Curly,
playing a waiter, enters his place of employment, the restaurant owner says, "Hello, Beau Brummel," and then slaps and
kicks him. All the players in the film behave the same way,
although there is still much speculation as to whether this is
the Stooges' stylized vision of a perfect world or how they
figured the world actually was.)

Certainly the rough-and-tumble, unflourished style of the
Stooges had its effect on Ernest Hemingway, as did the
Stooges' prolific use of lion-hunting and bullfighting imagery.
But do they teach you that in school? Hah, don't make me
laugh. If schoolteachers let kids know half of what's going on
in the world of lit, the kids would slit their throats and burn
down the schoolhouse. Howard, Fine, and Howard set the tone

for other Hemingway followers with shorts like *Loco Boy Makes Good*, in which the Stooges become involved with sexual strife and political rebellion in a Central American dictatorship. You'd have to be a real punk to miss how this part of *Loco Boy* was inspiration for Robert Stone's acclaimed *A Flag for Sunrise*, while the strange imagery of a white horse that picks up the Stooges as they face Latin death was repeated in *Under the Volcano*.

There has always been one school of American writing that was able to achieve only this first half (the Hemingway half) of the Stooges' style. These writers seek to be as tough as Moe but are unable to marry that toughness to a Curlyesque musicality. A recent example of that half-Stoogeliness is Jack Henry Abbott, whose *In the Belly of the Beast* was greatly influenced by the Stooges' prison movies and whose personal demeanor was greatly influenced by Moe's. Jack Henry undoubtedly heard the Stooges mutter, "Reminds me of reform school," in one of those ritzy mansions and was overwhelmed with verisimilitude.

Poor sap.

Abbott's patron, Norman Mailer, has himself acted out more than a few Stoogely skits, including being madly pursued by battalions of cops (*Armies of the Night*) and scared out of his wits by a big lion (*The Fight*). Norman has also tried to approximate Stoogely behavior at several hoity-toity dinner parties and once went after one of his wives with the sort of gusto we usually associate with Moe after he's been poked in the eye. The Mailer/Stooges connection could be explored further, but those of us traveling the Manhattan literary cocktail circuit try not to pee in our own stew, if you know what I mean.

To prove they were not as limited as their imitators, the Stooges explored other literary styles of their time. In *If a Body Meets a Body*, they took an Agatha Christie drawing room murder mystery and imbued it with a depth of characterization lacking in the old Jickey broad's jigsaw puzzle entertainments. Christie would have populated the yarn with wooden characters speaking elocution lessons. The Stooges gave us populist poetry. Where Agatha would have settled for a simple "Hush," Moe said, "If you so much as breathe, I'll tear your tonsils out and tie 'em around your neck for a bow tie!" Lady A. would have written, "Dim the light, will you Chadwick?" Moe substituted the far more gripping, "Blow out the candle, or I'll blow out your brains."

But if all they'd done was show up mystery writers, Moe, Larry, and Curly would not have been the OK jokers and great men of letters they were. These guys weren't just in it for weekends; they were integral to this century's most serious literary movements. And if you want proof of that, check out the haunting sequence in the Stooges-authored *Punch Drunks*, which Stooges scholars refer to as "Larry in Moe-Town."

At the time the Stooges conceived of this vehicle for Larry (some say the quiet Stooge was in fact the inspiration for Joyce's Jew, Leo Bloom), *Ulysses* was a recent text too risqué for the bourgeoisie and too dense for the public. Left to the cruel caprices of fate, the book most likely would have been out of print within three years, remaindered, and forgotten by 1940. Luckily for Joyce, the Stooges had the capacity of great minds to sense kindred spirits and weren't demeaned by the jealousies that diminish lesser talents. So they decided to give Joyce a boost by bringing his acid vision to the screen.

Fascinating as the possibility of a full-blown Stooges film version of *Ulysses* was, geniuses like Moe and the boys could not subjugate their artistic vision to Joyce's for the length of time it would take to make a full-length motion picture. Instead the Stooges tossed J.J.'s best notions into a blender with their own muse-powered inspiration and came out with one of the eeriest, most evocative passages in all Stoogedom. *Punch Drunks* is a short about Curly's career as a boxer (more Mailer influence here). The film proceeds according to a traditional ("rising action") structure until a point close to the climax. Then surrealism disrupts the surface of the narrative as a dream disrupts the order of our waking impressions. (No doubt the boys were doing some opiate in the days they spliced this one together.) Suddenly it becomes imperative that Larry find a radio playing "Pop Goes the Weasel." To that end he runs, clad as something close to a Hasidic rabbi, through the dark night streets of a completely deserted city. The only evidence of any life at all is an ancient radio, sitting on a sidewalk, blasting "Pop Goes the Weasel." Larry gathers the radio in his arms and carries it—unplugged but still playing— back to the arena, where the music dies. Again and again he returns to the empty city, each time trying to bring the music back to the crowd and each time losing his muse just as he finds the audience.

The public may not have understood *Larry in Moe-Town*, but they trusted the Stooges enough to allow themselves to experience its dream vision. Countless debates in classrooms and coffee houses raged over the meaning of the dream, but the one unconfused result was that Joyce's obscure *Ulysses* suddenly seemed not so strange and at least worth the effort of exploring. During the time *Punch Drunks* was being shown in theaters and on television, *Ulysses* went from being an arcane and perhaps obscene curio to a recognized classic. Coincidence? Sure. Just like the "coincidence" that the Nazis left France right after the Americans landed.

(One young man devoted to both James Joyce and the Three Stooges was that Irish Protestant Samuel Beckett, whose *Waiting for Godot* is a well-intentioned but ultimately uninspired bit of Three Stooges slapstick. If there's any doubt that the two vaudeville simpletons waiting like Job for a job are based on Moe and Larry, it is dispelled when they bring in the guy who's used as a horse—Curly's role in at least seven different Stooges shorts. Unable to mount an American production of his play before Curly's death, Beckett had to settle for Bert Lahr, the same actor who played the *Wizard of Oz*'s cowardly lion in full Curly style—right down to the "woowoo-woowoowoo" run down the corridor and window-crashing high dive. Beckett wasn't a *bad* playwright, but he was too much of a Stooge-worshipper ever to break free of their influence. Kind of like Brian De Palma's Hitchcock problem. Anyway, Beckett had a thing for heroes. He used to wear shoes so small they hurt his feet because that was the size shoe James Joyce wore. Many of the flat-topped dramatist's friends suspect he also wore trousers that came to just below his knee because that was Moe's pant-length.)

But please don't think Howard, Fine, and Howard were always dead serious in their scholarship! No, no, they could bust beans with the best of 'em. Look at how they'd tweak the noses of lesser-lit lights like Fitzgerald and Tolkien by naming characters Gatsby (*Violent Is the Word for Curly*) or Bilbo (*A Plumbing We Will Go*).

The Stooges' influence on modern literature was great indeed, but unlike their more shortsighted protégés, Curly and company never lost their love for the classics. This is significant because so many young kids today feel there's no use even trying to accomplish anything in literature—whatever you could try to do, the Stooges have already done. Well, here's a little secret, sweethearts: Curly and the cats had their heroes, too. And they paid tribute to them even as they improved on them, like in *Knutzy Knights*, when they stand beneath a maiden's balcony and woo her for her shy suitor. It's an obvious reference to *Cyrano*, just as modern drama's full of references to the Howards.

And I can hear you asking each other, "Who was the Stooges' biggest literary hero, then?" Well, of course, it was Shakespeare, that great dead writer who gave fools a good name.

References to the Bard dot the Howards' work like pockmarks on the countenance of art. Moe's mule in *Yes We Have No Bonanza* is named Yoric, and when the ass meets its doom, Moe's soliloquy on the nature of mortality is no less touching than Hamlet's. (In *Matri Phony*, the Stooges assume the role of Hamlet's uncle, pouring poison into a victim's gaping orifice while he sleeps in the garden.) In *Goofs and Saddles*, the boys take their cue from *MacBeth* sneaking up on their enemies while disguised as trees.

One of the Stooges' strangest allusions to Shakespeare is in *Movie Maniacs*, when Larry (who occasionally seemed to forget which script they were shooting that day) creeps up behind Curly, embraces him, and says romantically, "Kiss me, my Caliban!" (Those whose interest perks up here should turn to Chapter 5, on sexual mores.)

But the greatest example of the Stooges' devotion to the Durang of Avon was *Woman Haters*, the plot of which was a sort of second draft of *Love's Labour's Lost*. The notion of a

group of male friends who vow to each other to avoid dames—
and have a hard time doing so—was kept alive only in monas-
teries from Shakespeare's day until the Stooges revived it.
Like Shakespeare, the Stooges cast their play in poetry,
thereby upping the ante in their poker game with immortality,
and leading us into a new realm of their powerful influence.

3
The Stooges as Poets

ALTHOUGH THE THREE Stooges influenced modern poetry, it would be an exaggeration to imply that they were the sole or greatest influence on modern poetry—and one thing this volume can never be accused of is exaggeration. No, while Curly, Larry, and Moe did triple-handedly bring about the sexual revolution, modern painting, and more than a few other innovations outlined in other chapters, in poetry they were *part* of a movement that included other great twentieth-century voices. Sure they were at the vanguard, but they were not alone there. Their fellow modernists—poetic stooges all—were marching by the Howards' side.

Moe, Larry, and Curly were born into a world where sing-song sentimental verse was still recited at the hearthside, and schoolchildren learned to memorize "The Boy Stood on the Burning Deck" before they were toilet-trained. But as small children, the brilliant trio were probably exposed to the writing of William Butler Yeats, and as men they were part of a movement that included such peers as T. S. Eliot, e. e. cummings, and Ezra ("Rats Used to Come Out of This Hole") Pound.

As in so much else, the Stooges took a movement that was confined to academic backwashes and Cambridge wienie joints and brought it to a broad public.

In their approach to poetry, though, the Stooges were not of one instinct. Moe and Larry were inclined more toward formal structure and a subservience to strict meter that echoed that of Robert Frost. Curly, by contrast, sought to break down the walls of tight structure and free poetry to rush, ebb, and flow like life itself.

Here's an example of a Curly poem:

> Roses are red
> and how do you do
> Drink four of these
> and woowoowoowoo

Simple as this is to the uneducated eye, the scholar can detect a world of nuance beneath this placid surface. This is a pound of dynamite baked in an apple pie. Curly's launch point is a familiar bit of doggerel. But as soon as the reader thinks he can feel safe, as soon as he thinks he is on familiar ground, Curly pulls the rug out from under him. No sooner has "Roses are red" lulled the audience into false security than the poet yanks the rug out by varying from the anticipated "Violets are blue" with a substitution that not only upsets convention (any substitution would) but actually draws the reader in with a question aimed not at a character in the poem but at the reader himself! How disconcerting this must have been for a sentimental audience used to being flattered by the poet's treatment of them as omniscient observers! Curly figuratively reached out from the page and yanked the reader in, not with an invitation but with a challenge.

Clearly this was not reading for the winter fireside. This was a slap in the face to poetic convention. The work continues, "Drink four of these"—risqué perhaps, in introducing such rowdy behavior into a proper exercise, but not structurally radical. The reader, disconcerted by the second line, may begin to slip back into the confidence of a driver on a familiar road. But then—an explosion! Language itself breaks down and, with "woowoowoowoo" the poet unleashes a rapid-fire flatulence of oral exhilaration. The *woowoo*'s have no obvious end—there is no stop to mark a firm border between the territory of the poem and our own reality. Rather, the circular, unending "woowoowoo" may be stretched like chewing gum, may reach beyond any sense of meter or rhyme, of the confines of structure. Here, so much better than in William Carlos Williams's overvalued "So much depends upon a red wheelbarrow," poetry makes claim to its ability to be a thing untamed, a force not easy to control. How like Curly himself!

By contrast, let us examine the poetry of the other Stooges *without* Curly. These examples come from shorts in which Shemp was the third Stooge:

> Good morn to thee fair princess
> Weep not or you'll get bags
> We come to bring thee laughter
> With buffoonery and gags

Here is the sort of conservatism that made Frost so popular with readers of family magazines. Note the supplicating tone, the imploring of good intentions, and the antiquated invocation of courtliness. Sure, the Stooges without Curly were capable of a certain rowdiness:

> In days of old
> when knights were bold
> the guys were hot
> but the girls were cold

and:

> Unhand my lass
> you brazen ass

For all the shock value of such lines, there was no challenge to or expansion of the form of poetry itself. Even Moe's efforts at surrealism ("Oh the cows were flying about/As the wife made sauerkraut") were tied to traditional structures; only the imagery was fresh. But this should not be surprising. For all the Stooges' poetic instincts were laid out in their earliest short, the groundbreaking *Woman Haters*. Here we find not only the origins of Moe, Larry, and Curly's versifying instincts, but evidence of how their imperatives shaped a generation.

Written entirely in verse, *Woman Haters* finds Moe and Curly threatening Larry with a gusto that celebrates the inebriating lilt of song, while hinting at the dark complexities of friendship, loyalty, and mortality.

>   *Moe:* If you violate the rules
>   of the club you're just
>   as good as dead
>   *Curly:* If you get married
>   You'll be carried
>   Out and plonked right
>   On the head

Here Curly takes Moe's established meter, bends it out of shape, finesses him by dropping in an interior rhyme at the top, and then delivers the touché by pulling out of his nosedive to provide a rhyme of his own for the line Moe left dangling. A virtuoso performance, and one that walks out on poetry's wing only to land with both feet on the ground. Others may think Curly's bravest Stooge stunts were hanging off cliffs or falling into wells, but the academic recognizes that those feats of courage pale beside this sort of daredevil poeticizing.

Sometimes Curly's tweaks of Moe's meter got more blatant. Listen to this exchange:

>   *Moe:* To the Three Musketeers
>   Who stuck together for years
>   We traveled together
>   In every kind of weather

It's all a little too clichéd, sentimental, and grandiose for Curly, who prepares to extract vengeance:

>   *Moe:* Say, by the way,
>   Don't we leave for the road tonight?
>   *Curly:* What day is this?
>   *Moe:* The twenty-first.
>   *Curly:* By golly, you're right!

What a shot! Moe was livid! Here was Moe grinding away beneath the self-imposed yoke of strict meter, getting off his little internal rhyme at the top, and at the very end Curly upsets the metric applecart by introducing a *contraction*! In violation of every ancient rule, Curly drops a syllable, not because he has to, but because he wants to! "You are right" would have scanned perfectly, but instead Curly went for the vernacular. In doing so, he provoked the rage of his brother and every other traditionalist, but in doing so he also inspired a generation of poets to cast aside the old constrictions and speak as men impassioned by their calling.

Note in this next example how Curly uses a stilted meter to dramatic effect, throwing off expectations to delay and create tension in the structure:

> You stay where you are
> I'll find out what's goin' on
> In the next car

Interestingly, Curly—whose love of jazz rhythms influenced his ear—then passes a black porter, who recites:

> Sho' nuff
> He's in there with a lady
> And brother
> Is she hot stuff

Moe, with his barely contained violence and formal deference to poetic tradition, might have inspired Pound (whose "Goodly Freer" cast Christ as a finger-poking, face-slapping slapstick Messiah), but Pound, whose administrative ideas also paralleled Moe's, ended up in the nuthouse. Curly was perhaps more to the liking of Eliot, who beneath his formal facade was also interested in chipping away at the constraints of rigid structure. But Eliot, like the post-Curly Stooges, finally slipped into a comfortable conservatism.

The poet most clearly descended from Curly, then, must be e. e. cummings, whose vavavavoom never deserted him and whose elegy to "Buffalo Bill" is assumed by some academics to be a homage to Curly (in his *Goofs and Saddles* persona).

The influence of Curly on modern poems like "Howl" goes without saying.

So we are left, as our century draws toward its close, with a legacy of poetic innovation spurred on by the rivalry of different movements and given voice in the battle songs of a revolution against the old order. That Moe and Larry could not carry the poetic banner as far or raise it as high as Curly is no dishonor to them. For still their gifts were great, and still they advanced far. But next time your heart is lifted by "Ash Wednesday" or the "Ode to a Blackbird," hold your horses a moment and think kindly of Curly Howard. Without him we might all still be standing on the burning deck.

4
The Relationship of the Three Stooges to Sigmund Freud

HOW DIFFERENT A world we inhabit from that through which our grandparents walked! As we approach the end of the twentieth century, it's easy to lose sight of the strange, dark lives lived by those young when this century was new. Oh, we have our AIDS and herpes, our toxic waste and atom bombs. But what are these next to the consumption, the cholera, the polio, all the plagues that chased our forebears up and down the staircases of 1900? Even those with operable illnesses had no safe anesthesia; even those with primitive automobiles had no windshields.

Imagine this strange and frightening world, where royalty still ruled the great nations and inbred till international policies were as retarded as their own offspring. Imagine two homes, a world apart and yet united by ancient culture and impending destiny. Imagine, in Vienna, the home of the Freuds, and in New York the home of the Howards.

They were as different as an ancient heritage and an immigrant culture, as different as academic study and the enterprise of street urchins. The two homes were as different as the dark nighttime knock of repression and the sunny afternoon shouts of democracy.

Yet how much these two breeding grounds had in common. For the house of Freud and the home of Howard shared, more than the reproof of ignorant neighbors, the stuff of greatness.

Photo courtesy Wide World Photos.

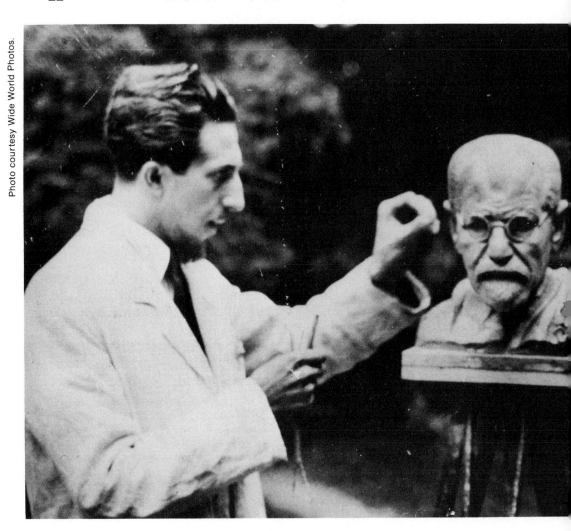

When the names of the scoffers, the insulters, the self-righteous and complaining upholders of dusty morals were forgotten, how the new century would sing the names of Moe, of Curly, of Sigmund.

And though it was Freud who formulated the theories of psychotherapy, it was the Howards who would bring his wild insights to the understanding of the world. For without the Three Stooges, Sigmund Freud's name would today be known

The great man about
to get an eyeful of clay.

only to devout academics. It was the Stooges—Howard, Fine, and Howard—who gave his concepts flesh and fire. They were his Boswells; they were his St. Pauls. They spread Freud's gospel to the masses.

Freud—who may or may not have been a great fan of the Stooges, often skipping medical conferences to catch their early shorts—managed to distill his most important theory in the shape of the Stooges. The doctor claimed that the mind could be divided into three parts: the ego, the superego, and the id. The Great Man then sat back and smiled. But the world responded not with accolades, but with a resounding "Huh?"

> "Step aside," Moe Howard piped up. "I'll explain it so even *you* can understand.
>
> "Think of it this way: Larry, the regular guy, is the **ego**, trying to mind his own business and maybe catch a free meal, a quick date, or a good horse race.
>
> "Curly represents the **id**, an uninhibited caldron of wild desires, frenzied motion, and primal ambition. Left to his own devices, Curly would probably eat the tablecloth and marry the racehorse.
>
> "That's why you need me, Moe, the **superego**, slapping the others into shape and repressing all their primal desires. It's me who stops Curly from leading Larry into profligate enterprise and wanton mischief. It's the superego that slaps the id in the kisser before it convinces the ego to go for the gusto."

Each of us has within him a Curly, telling us to cut loose, and a Moe, jabbing us back into place. We try to be good Larrys but one extra Curly chromosome here and—poof—you're Henry VIII, feeding your indulgences all day long. One extra Moe chromosome and—snap—you're J. Edgar Hoover, repressing yourself and everybody else to the point of constipation.

Once the Stooges recognized themselves as Freud's evangelists, they took to their proselytizing with enthusiasm. Even *Herr Doktor* might have been shaken by the scene in *Dutiful but Dumb* in which Moe sticks an old-fashioned accordionlike camera through a transom to spy on a couple about to consummate their relationship. "Oh, darling!" cries the man. "This is the supreme moment!" and Moe's camera shoots out, unfolding like a wild libido.

For while Freud understood, the Stooges acted—and in acting paved the way for a revolution in modern sexual mores.

5
The Influence of the Stooges on Sexual Mores

WESTERN SOCIETY HAS always tried to hide sex under the bed, but in the last fifty years it's refused to stay put. To some degree this boldness may be attributable to the rumble seat, flappers, the experiences of the GIs in Europe during World War II, women working, rock 'n' roll music, the birth control pill, the breakdown of the nuclear family, feminism, gay activism, and the new adrogyny—but most of the credit must go to the Three Stooges.

Back in the days when a glimpse of shoulder was considered shocking and the knee was an erogenous zone, Moe, Larry, and Curly set out to dismantle the barriers between man and woman—and, for that matter, between man and man. Their subtlety protected them from arrest, but their impact was enormous. The Three Stooges were the founding fathers of the sexual revolution. They manifested at different times a chastity bordering on sexual hysteria; the sort of macho sexual swagger that Hugh Hefner made a fortune propagating in the 1950s; homosexuality; and, finally, a complete annihilation of gender distinctions, complete with cross-dressing and the trading of sex roles. Heady stuff for its time, the effects of the Stooges' erotic trailblazing are still shaking society today.

Let us first examine the earliest stage of the Stooges' sexual development. Hard as it is to believe of such notorious romantic pioneers, Howard, Fine, and Howard were capable of displaying an adolescent's romantic jitters. In *Movie Maniacs*, a beautiful starlet throws herself at Moe, expecting a kiss. Moe becomes flustered and can barely summon the courage to peck her on the cheek. Next she moves to Larry, who reacts with the same inexperienced humility. The starlet then grabs Curly, sweeps him back, and kisses him passionately. He goes into convulsions, falling to the floor, shaking and screaming in erotic lunacy.

Reminds me of *The White Hotel*.

But soon the Stooges were able to outgrow this pubescent Chaplin nonsense and express a heterosexual boldness rare in its day. "Come on, baby," a swaggering Curly enjoins a cute French maid. "Tell me, do you live alone or with your folks? And if alone, what are you doing tonight?"

No mistaking the rotund Romeo's motives there. And there's no missing how far the Stooges have strayed from the path of chastity when, in *Dizzy Pilots*, Larry tells Moe he's "as pure as the driven snow." "Yeah," says Moe, slapping him, "but you drifted."

Further evidence of Larry's sexual bravado is displayed in *Goofs and Saddles*, when he walks into a saloon, grabs the hat off the head of a fellow talking to a dancing girl, and tosses it away. As soon as the competitor chases after his hat, Larry slides up to the dancer and coos, "Where you been all my life?"

This sort of swaggering, macho sexuality was picked up a decade later by Marlon Brando in *Streetcar Named Desire* and in the early *Playboy*. It kept Henry Miller on the disabled list.

Once the Stooges discovered debauchery, there was no stopping them. In *Termites of 1938*, they run a male escort service, and in *Wee Wee Monsieur*, they abandon their plan to free a captive from an evil sheik when they discover his harem. The Stooges dive into the bevy of scantily clad concubines like Johnny Weismuller into an Olympic pool, adding group sex to their list of exercises.

In the 1970s, Warren Beatty's *Shampoo* created controversy without ever getting that far gone, and Harold Robbins minted money with a similar formula.

The Howards' sexual boldness reached an epitome in *Pop Goes the Easel* when Curly approached a pretty ballerina and

Even interracial transexual dancing was no taboo to the ribald Curly. Photo courtesy Columbia Pictures Corporation.

asked if she would do him a favor. No sooner had the poor young woman said yes than the lumpy Lothario grabbed her by the ankles and turned her upside down.

Even fifty years later, this scene brings on a blush. When an older Brando *approached* this level of sexual frankness with *Last Tango in Paris* in the early seventies, critics declared it revolutionary.

Given all this profligacy, it's not surprising that the Stooges were no respecters of the covenant of marriage. Indeed, when Larry is asked in *Easel* for a bridge-playing tip, he responds to the innocent query, "What would you do if you held the queen alone?" with a leering, "That depends on what time the king's expected home."

By the time of *What's the Matador* in 1941, the Stooges weren't even worried about the husbands. They took great pleasure in attempting to seduce a married woman while her husband slept. Once discovered, they made good their own escape and left the discarded woman to her husband's rage.

Curly, Larry, and Moe's progressive attitudes toward marriage were outlined in 1940's *Boobs in Arms*. The Stooges, working as salesmen, suggest a young bride buy a gift for her husband *or* her sweetheart, implying that of course she has both. The young woman complains that her husband no longer loves her.

"Is that all?" Larry scoffs. "I thought it was serious. That's easily fixed!"

"Why certainly," Moe adds, with the gusto of a true sinner. "All you have to do is get somebody to make love to you and make your husband jealous!"

Curly is designated cuckolder, and the young bride jumps into his lap and starts kissing him. This sort of extramarital territory is still rarely explored in art or entertainment without the character's paying a severe price in the end. Only D. H. Lawrence has dared to second the Stoogely suggestion that adultery can be fun and painless. And it kept him out of the bookstores for a long, long time.

In *Three Missing Links*, the Stooges venture into a lost jungle and find a potent aphrodisiac. The witch doctor, a big black fellow with a bone through his nose, promises that "Love candy make strong love!" and later makes the rather lewd suggestion that if "me give you love candy, you give me nice big bone!"

Armed with his herbal romance enhancer, Curly sets off to seduce a beautiful young woman, but ends up falling for a gorilla. This flirtation with bestiality is as unexpected as it is blatant, as Curly chases the frightened ape while crowing, "Darling, I love ya! Give me a little kiss, baby! Wait for poppa!"

Clearly the Stooges were pushing their erotic explorations into uncharted territory. In the same short, Moe lies in bed while a lion licks his feet. He thinks it's Curly doing the licking and expresses uncharacteristic glee.

The Stooges' explorations of homoerotic behavior started carefully and then burst out into the open. When Moe and Curly embraced each other in a crashing plane in *Dizzy Pilots*, Larry leered, "Do you guys go steady?" In the same way, *Some More of Samoa* opens with the Stooges trying to find a reason a rare tree won't bear fruit. "This tree needs a girlfriend," announces Moe. "Or maybe a boyfriend," giggles Curly, as Moe glares.

In *Oily to Bed, Oily to Rise*, Curly sweeps up his fiancée, leans forward, and kisses Moe. In *Micro-Phonies*, the Stooges get so excited at the sound of beautiful music that they kiss each other.

These subtle hints at the Stooges' fascination with the Sin That Dare Not Speak Its Name soon bloomed into blatancy. "If at first you don't succeed," Curly suggested in *Movie Maniacs*, "keep on sucking till you do suck seed!" In the same seminal short, the Stooges climb into bed together not in their usual side-by-side position, but with Moe and Larry facing north and Curly between them facing south. Clearly the boys were intent on pressing the standards of public morality and the license of the Hays Office to their limits.

By the end of *Movie Maniacs*, Larry, Moe, and Curly have crossed over altogether, as Curly dons a blonde wig and ball gown to take the place of a glamorous actress, and Larry becomes his/her suitor. It's not the only time the Stooges will transvest and couple. In *Uncivil Warriors*, Curly dresses as a woman to pose as Moe's wife, no sooner crossing the sexual border than screeching, "Darling! Kiss me!"

In *Pop Goes the Easel*, Curly gets off a legal hook by dressing up as Mae West and flirting with the policeman who's been pursuing him. "How are ya, tall and handsome?" Curly croons. "I'm glad ya came up to *see* me." A moment later Larry and Moe, also dressed in women's clothes, come flirting in to join the orgy.

Who can say how much this erotic evolution—from nervous chastity to heterosexual aplomb to all manner of homoerotic hanky-panky—affected the small children who watched the

Stooges in the darkened movie theaters of the Depression and the bright screens of the television era? What ideas, from Bob Guccione to Boy George, were formed by different aspects of the Stooges' sexual explorations?

Remember that telling scene at the conclusion of *Calling All Curs* when the Stooges find Garson the canine in the closet of the thieves who dognapped him? Curly and the boys open the door to find that Garson has given birth—that the male dog is in fact a bitch. As that dog came out of his closet, so did the Stooges' generation.

6
The Relation of the Stooges to the New Deal

WHEN RONALD REAGAN was president of the Screen Actors Guild, he helped push through a ruling that the residuals paid actors for old films shown on television would be paid out only for movies made after the 1950s. Thus did the future president screw the Three Stooges out of the fortunes they could have earned from the great popularity of their old shorts on TV. Thus did Reagan consign Larry to the Old Actors Home.

What else could the Stooges expect from a Republican? The political subtext of Moe, Larry, and Curly's work, while obvious to scholars and vengeful GOP leaders, might be missed by those students whose knowledge of American government is limited to *Rocky* movies, high school social studies courses, and John Cougar records. But to those familiar with the historic battle for the heart of this nation, the Stooges stand as the last lonely voice crying for the traditional Democratic coalition. Walter Mondale, Gary Hart, and Ted Kennedy may struggle to keep the old spark lit, but in the hands of Curly, Larry, and Moe that flame became an incandescent blowtorch, sizzling through the reinforced walls of Republican selfishness.

The very first Three Stooges short, *Woman Haters*, opened with an NRA seal and the proud inscription "We Do Our Part." Then the Stooges' faces appeared. Thus, in the brief pause before diving into the whirlpool of comedic chaos that was to be their destiny and legacy, Howard, Fine, and Howard took an instant to state unequivocally that their hearts were with Franklin Roosevelt's then-controversial National Relief Agency.

From then on the Stooges' political devotion became more subtle, if no less impassioned. How much of the Stoogely mythos was a direct result of—an acerbic comment on—the Depression? How many shorts opened with Curly, Larry, and Moe hungry for food and work, chewing on their dirty hats while rich men feasted behind restaurant glass?

Cash and Carry opened with the destitute Stooges crawling toward California in a rickety old truck packed with all their belongings. The obvious reference to *The Grapes of Wrath* was not lost on John Steinbeck, whose own migration toward Hollywood paralleled the Howards' and who has never been alleged not to have been a devoted Three Stooges enthusiast.

The Stooges, in *Cash and Carry*, make their home in a dump (a dirty "Hooverville") where they find a crippled orphan boy and his sister scrounging pennies for an impossibly expensive leg operation. When the Stooges learn that the little boy keeps his meager savings in a tin can, Moe (whose innate sense of compassion rarely found opportunity for expression in the company of Larry and Curly) asks, "Why don't you put your money in the bank?" The child replies with a question of his own: "Will the bank give it back to us?"

"They didn't used to," Curly pipes up, his effervescent aplomb belied by the bitterness of his words, "but now they do."

Thus were thousands of skeptical Americans reassured about the trustworthiness of the newly formed FDIC.

When the Stooges go to the bank, though, they are rebuffed by a clerk and swindled by a crook, both of whom resemble, from mustache to Wildroot sheen, GOP leader Thomas Dewey. Now what does this mean in the context of the time? Dewey, the slick-haired New Yorker, was the Republicans' great hope for returning to power. Whenever there's a cruel banker, mortgage grabber, claim jumper, or dispossessor of widows and orphans in a Stooges short, he resembles Tom Dewey.

Photo courtesy Columbia Pictures Corporation.

That biting and sustained innuendo may be lost on today's historically illiterate viewers, but in the context of the Stooges' time it was a shattering indictment—a Swiftian satirical kick with the cumulative effect of pulling a "guaranteed" presidential election away from Dewey after Roosevelt's death.

"How long have you been starving?" a Dewey look-alike asks Curly in one short.

"Mister," Curly says, "I haven't tasted food in three days."

"Well, I wouldn't worry about it," laughs the Republican. "It still tastes the same!"

Although the Stooges tried to keep their political loyalties from dominating their work, they could not resist the occasional outright endorsement. In *Back to the Woods*, the boys were pilgrims cast in a Republican, property-obsessed New World.

Thomas Dewey, Republican hero, Nixon mentor, and the kind of guy who would have hired the Stooges to fix his plumbing and end up attacking them with hammers and pick handles. Photo courtesy UPI/Bettmann Newsphotos.

"No hunting, no swimming, no camping," Curly moaned. "And they call this the land of liberty." A better hope? Here the partisan side of Howard, Fine, and Howard could not contain itself. "I need not charity!" Larry boasted. "I'm on the WPA! Willing Pilgrim Association."

More than an endorsement of another Roosevelt program, Larry's association of FDR's WPA with the pilgrims' Plymouth Compact was a direct challenge to—and refutation of—every Republican who accused Roosevelt's New Deal of introducing un-American socialism to the nation. Larry's biting comment made the point that socialism in its pure state arrived on the Mayflower, that the social cooperation and limited economic redistribution of the New Deal was—far from the radical departure the Republicans alleged—a reassertion of a value rich in American tradition.

Which contemporary Democrat would go so far?

In a way, Roosevelt and the Stooges acted as a team. FDR devising the plays and carrying the ball while Moe, Larry, and Curly made clear his path.

The Stooges explained complex New Deal policies in a way the public could understand. It is surely more than coincidence that the only U.S. president to enjoy the enthusiastic endorsement of the Three Stooges was also the only president elected four times.

Could FDR have succeeded without the Stooges? That's like asking if Lincoln could have avoided the disasters of Reconstruction, like asking if God can make a rock so big He can't lift it, if Dick York made a better Darren than Dick Sargent. Philosophers and scholars will debate such questions as long as there are curriculums to pad and public access cable channels. But this much is sure: however it might have gone without the combination of FDR and ML&C, together they pulled America out of a Depression and back to prosperity.

"Last one in is a Republican," cried the happy young bride in *Three Sappy People*, and the Stooges raced to head her off.

And when, in the seminal *Cash and Carry*, the Stooges found themselves imprisoned for breaking into the U.S. Treasury to finance the little orphan boy's leg operation, who was it who descended like Deus in the machina to approve this redistribution of the wealth and socialization of medicine? It was Franklin Roosevelt himself!

"I'm sorry, gentlemen," says a presidential aide to a group of dignitaries. "The Senate subcommittee will have to wait. The president is in conference."

Inside the oval office, FDR grants the Stooges executive clemency and assures the little crippled boy he'll arrange for his operation "poissonally."

"Gosh, Mister President," Curly declares, striking a smile and a salute, "You're a swell guy!"

No political endorsement was ever more sincere—and none more effective.

7
Post-Stooge Morality in Fiction and Drama *or* Listen to Your Mentors!

LARRY: Five hundred dollars!
  MOE: Who do we have to moider?
Micro-Phonies

IN THE LATE 1970s, novelist John Gardiner spoke up about the need for "moral fiction," a petition greeted with grunts and chortles by his peers among contemporary writers, who had enough trouble coming up with books without any constraints on their natural inclinations. Shortly after his cry for morality, Gardiner was dead under circumstances that could be called "unnatural." The connection? Let's just say that morality has little place in the popular culture of the post-Stoogely society. When Howard, Fine, and Howard portrayed themselves as cowardly, greedy, and dim strivers, they broke with all the conventions of drama. Now we see the generation of authors and dramatists who grew up absorbing the Stooges turn the literature of America into a Xerox machine, spewing out variations on the work of Curly, Larry, and Moe with no improvement on the original product.

Perhaps the difference between the sublime (Stooges) and the obscene (today's copycats) is that the Stooges always had some spark of human decency threatening to illuminate the dark night of their sleazy ambitions. Sure, they lived in a dump and greedily pocketed the money they found hidden there. (Many of Sam Shepard's plays proceed from a similar premise.) But even Moe's heart was human enough to return the moola when he found out it belonged to the crippled

37

orphan boy. This strain of decency amid the squalor survived into early Stooge-influenced works like *Of Mice and Men*.

But today that light has gone out, leaving only the rotten. What can one say about the dimestore nihilism of a best-seller like Jay McInerney's *Bright Lights, Big City* in which the narrator dribbles away 182 pages describing how miserable and debauched he is with an eye to detail that suggests the aid of a demographic breakdown of the book-buying audience? This can be said: Curly Howard might have gone to the nightclub, gotten plastered, danced with all the wrong women, set the rodent loose in the boss's office, and accidentally knocked out the fellow next door (as the hero in *Bright Lights* does), but Curly would not have whined about how miserable it all made him. Curly would have just lammed out of there with no pretensions to tragedy and a gaggle of cops on his trail.

Been to a Broadway show lately? Serious theater has become a lavatory wall upon which the black-hearted playwright scrawls obscene graffiti and repeats the Three Stooges' innovations until they become clichés. David Mamet's protagonists plan scams and petty thefts like Moe on a bad day.

What would Mamet give for a plot as rich (or an inclination as perverse) as the Stooges displayed in *Calling All Curs*? Fly-by-night veterinarians, the boys allow an old woman's beloved dog to be stolen and attempt to cover for themselves by disguising another dog and trying to pass it off. "The old lady won't know the difference," Moe claims, with a cynicism *American Buffalo* or *Glengarry Glen Ross* strive for but never achieve. When the Stooges do agree to help find the missing pooch, it's not out of any generosity; it's only to stay out of jail.

Even *Sweeney Todd*, Stephen Sondheim's celebration of murder and cannibalism, owed much of its aplomb to the sort of ear-ripping, throat-cutting, dismembering enthusiasm Moe's threats made acceptable to a mass audience. It's hard for the knowledgeable critic to sit through *Sweeney Todd* without recalling Curly's own barbershop manner: "Say," he asked, straight razor flying, "were you wearing a pink bow tie? No? Then here's your lip."

In David Rabe's *Hurly Burly*, a trio of disreputable characters spent three endless acts attempting the sort of debauchery that Curly, Moe, and Larry could have achieved in a single reel. The play's supporters find satirical merit in its jibes at the Hollywood mentality. But even those jibes are nothing Stooges fans won't recognize as Howardisms.

In *Movie Maniacs* (1935), Moe defended the Stooges' right to make films, saying "There's a couple of thousand people in pictures now who know nothin' about it—three more won't make no difference." More pointed is the sign that greets studio visitors in that short: "Carnation Pictures—From Contented Actors." Years later, Alfred Hitchcock would excite endless controversy by muttering, "Actors are cattle." As with so much, someone else got the credit for a clumsy repetition of a subtle Stoogely thought.

In the current theater, *Orphans* distills the Three Stooges plot to its essence. Two brothers, a Moelike older bully who considers himself the brains and a Curlyish childlike lout with a good heart and a tendency to bark like a dog, live together in an abysmal shack in lowdown poverty. Enter a smooth-talking big city gangster who involves them in a get-rich-quick scheme, which sees the boys trying, by the second act, to dress and conduct themselves as "gentlemen." Sound a little familiar? Any schoolchild would recognize the scenario as vintage Stooges. Unfortunately, today's theater critics are not schoolchildren.

What made the Three Stooges' upturning of traditional morality so remarkable is that they achieved it in a place (Hollywood) and at a time when the motion picture industry had actual provisions against the celebration of immorality, crime, or decadence. When the old motion picture code was scrapped in favor of the movie rating system in the late sixties, it was celebrated as the liberation of film from moral restrictions. A movie like Sam Peckinpah's *The Getaway* was considered revolutionary because the bank-robbing protagonists were not killed or captured in the final reel. How Moe Howard must have laughed at such revolutions! The Stooges had been getting away with moider for years!

Remember the time the boys thought they had killed someone, sacked and hoisted a mannequin (which they took to be

Jack Nicholson borrows the windblown hairstyle and charm of Larry Fine.

"the stiff") onto Curly's back, and snuck off to bury it where the cops would never find it? How come fifty years later Hollywood declares itself bold and groundbreaking when a *Prizzi's Honor** does the same thing? While director John Huston was still having his killers "take the fall," Moe and the boys were looking for a safe place to ditch the body.

---

*Note to film scholars: Jack Nicholson, star of *Prizzi's Honor*, is perhaps the most Stoogely of all contemporary Hollywood figures. *Goin' South*, in which Nicholson agreed to marry a local widow only to get out of being hanged, owed its very premise to the Howards, while *The Fortune* found a frizzy-haired, moron Nicholson doing a whole film in imitation of Larry Fine. Costar Warren Beatty was a bit less successful in trying to combine Moe and Shemp, but serious Stooges fans should dig out copies of *The Fortune* to see a rare example of Hollywood at least nodding to the Stooges as it copied them.

CURLY: Did you steal it?
LARRY: What do you think I am, a crook? I just took it.

Whoops, I'm an Indian

Robert Altman's 1970 film *McCabe and Mrs. Miller* was thought either to revitalize or to bury the western with its portrayal of a cardsharp hero in a miserable lumber camp. But the whole scenario was a rip-off of (perhaps French critics would call it a tribute to) *Whoops, I'm an Indian*, the seminal Stooges short in which Curly, Larry, and Moe are running a crooked crap game in a trapper's camp every bit as miserable as Altman's. And if Julie Christie's whore, Mrs. Miller, was shocking to audiences in 1970, how much more revolutionary was *Whoops*, in which Curly tried to dissuade a Canadian trapper from killing him by dressing as an Indian squaw and marrying him? There are few moments in modern cinema as charged with sexual energy as the instant when the lumberjack drags Curly off for "ze honeymoon" while leering, "For you I have ze *grand* surprise!"

Altman's previous great claim to fame was his direction of the film version of *M*A*S*H*, a movie considerably more grizzly and coldhearted than the sentimental TV show that followed. But even Altman's vision of Hawkeye and Trapper was *Doctor Kildare* when set against the Stooges' 1934 *Men in Black*. In that dark exploration of the medical profession, the Three Surgeons are brought before a suffering man. When they return to their superior, he asks, "What did you do for the patient?"

"Nothin'," Curly replies. "What did he ever do for us?"

John Gardiner didn't know what he was up against. In *Tassels in the Air* the Stooges got rid of their angry boss by opening an elevator shaft and letting him plunge to his death. At that moment the tradition of moral fiction had been dealt a death blow. Moe Howard opened the elevator shaft, and the old fiction (Faulkner, Fitzgerald) plunged in. This is the day of the half-true fictionalized glorification of the vile, of *In Cold Blood* and *The Executioner's Song*. How prescient seems that Stoogely sentimentality: "Our father drew twenty years with a stroke of the pen."

8
The Effects of the Three Stooges on the Ayatollah Khomeini

*T*HE AMERICAN STOOGE *Symposium received the following submission from Shemp Shinome of Teheran,
Iran. We have written to Ayatollah Khomeini to ascertain its authenticity, but have so far received no reply.*

I was with Khomeini when the American hostages flew to
West Germany. As the ayatollah and I strolled through the
debris of what was once the U.S. Embassy in Teheran, I said to
him, "Well, Imam, how do you figure it?"

"Shemp," the A.K. answered, kicking a dusty beer can across
the soiled carpet, "I thought they'd *never* leave."

I should explain up front that Shemp is not my real name. It
is an Islamic name I adopted when I moved to Iran from New
Jersey in 1978. My real name is Sirhan. After years of being
strip-searched at airports, I had my name legally changed to
that of my favorite Stooge. This seemingly minor matter stood
me in good stead when I got to know the ayatollah. It turned
out that the man was a great fan of the Three Stooges and
based much of his own public image on Moe Howard. No
sooner had the Turbaned Titan heard my name than he
pressed me into service as his batman.

This story is about my work as Ayatollah Khomeini's butler.
Looking back, I suppose it was seeing the Stooges' *Malice in
the Palace* that started me thinking about returning to the
land of my ancestors. I was feeling down in the dumps, I had

43

broken off my engagement to a beautiful fashion model, I was feeling dyspeptic. Suddenly there were the Stooges, running amok at the "Cafe Casbahbah" and driving crazy Lassan Ben Sober, a turbaned, bearded mullah who looked an awful lot like Khomeini, who was at that time enjoying a long exile in France.

The Stooges seemed to understand a lot more about the Persian mentality than other Westerners. At a time when other Americans were kissing the shah's peacock throne, Moe and the boys saw through the false monarchy to the real Iran (a place they fixed on their map of the world next to Heran, Sheran, Theyran, and Alsoran). Howard, Fine, and Howard held out the possibility of the ancient order reemerging, of an Iran where turbaned ancients still chased white men around with scimitars.

Taking inspiration from *Malice*, I sold the little I had and returned to Persia just in time for the ousting of the shah. I got a job as a typist for a fanatical revolutionary group, and as soon as they found out I spoke French I was shoved into a delegation bound for Paris to plead with the ayatollah to return to Iran and consolidate the revolution.

A lot of people don't know exactly how Ruhollah Khomeini spent his long years of exile. Well, when I approached him in the south of France, the imam was dressed in a gray track suit and was puffing his way through a badminton match. It took some coaxing to get the old boy even to consider coming out of retirement to lead a country as nutty as Iran, but the delegates of the various political, religious, and cultural factions finally convinced the master mullah that this was a very lucrative figurehead position with only ceremonial duties.

"Remember when Moe was offered the chance to become a dictator?" I asked. "He jumped at the chance. Besides, you can bring all your Stooges tapes with you. You could even make them mandatory viewing on revolutionary TV." This appealed not only to the imam's cultural philanthropy, but also to his desire to have Moe's face available to him at all hours. He agreed to go home and try to establish the world's first truly Stoogely government.

At first the work in Teheran was pretty laid back. A fiery

speech here and there, but nothing strenuous. Mostly the A.K. stayed in his office and practiced putting into a little golf-ball-catching machine the shah had left behind. The imam was thus engrossed when word came that a bunch of militant students had captured the American Embassy.

"Tell them to give it back," suggested Khomeini, going for a birdie.

"It's not that simple, Holy One," I explained. "The students have broken international law and claimed this act as part of the revolution. It would be a humiliation in the eyes of the whole world for them to surrender now."

"And what if the goddamned U.S. marines come charging up the nearest sand dune equivalent of San Juan Hill?" Khomeini shouted. "Those bastards are crazy, you know!"

"Uhh . . ." I hated to be the bearer of bad tidings, especially in Iran. "I don't think they'll send in the marines, Imam."

"Why not, Shemp?"

"Uh, because, most High and Holy One, the students are holding some, um," I mumbled.

"What?"

"Some hostages, Imam "

"Some hostages?!"

I thought the ayatollah's turban was going to unwind right there.

"Yes, your idolatry. The American diplomats."

"How many?"

"I, um, I'm not sure exactly, Imam. Several."

"Ten?"

"More than ten, ayatollah."

"More than ten. Twenty?"

"Ahhh, I think around sixty, Holiness."

You may think you know anger, but let me clue you in, Jack. You don't know anger until you've tried shoving smelling salts up the nostrils of a livid ayatollah. Once his face faded to a light purple, Khomeini decided to head straight over to the embassy to sort matters out.

At this point I should explain something else about Ayatollah the K. A lot of you don't realize how he gets around Iran. The reason you don't know is because the man has hit upon a method more than a few Western celebrities would be wise to imitate. Whenever he appears officially, the Persian Poobah wears flowing black robes and a big black turban. You've probably seen pictures. That little ensemble is murder on hot Iranian afternoons, but it's worth it. Whenever the A.K. wants to get around anonymously he simply jumps into some white painter's pants, a pair of sunglasses, and a Moe wig. Thus garbed, he comes and goes as he pleases and the paparazzi never catch on.

Needless to say, Khomeini gave those student militants one hell of a tongue lashing. "I'll rip your lips off!" he screamed. "I'll reach down your throats and tear out your spines! I'll unzip your nostrils! I'll annihilate ya!"

Right in the middle of his harangue, the kids all fell to their knees and began bowing to Mecca. The imam was so furious that he walked around kicking their prostrated butts.

At that point the students got uppity and began talking back to the ayatollah. They said they'd let the women and blacks go, but the white male hostages had to stay. It didn't take Khomeini or me long to realize that the students' true goal was to humiliate America in the eyes of the world by forcing the middle-aged career diplomats to play Iran's best student athletes in the university homecoming game. The stalemate between Khomeini and the students lasted four weeks, during which the ayatollah put pressure on teachers to double the militants' homework until the hostages were turned over to the government.

That transfer took place, secretly, in December of 1979. As far as the A.K. and I were concerned, the hostages could have left anytime from then on. Why, then, did it take another thirteen months to get them home? Now it can be told: the hostages didn't want to leave.

Nothing Khomeini said could budge them. How well I remember the scene the morning after American rescue planes crashed in the desert. I drove the ayatollah to the embassy, where the Americans were munching caviar and watching the Stooges on the Betamax.

"This has gone far enough!" the imam screamed. "You people are eating us out of house and home, you're causing us trouble with the rest of the world, and now we've almost had an American invasion. Will you *please* go home?"

"No way, Aya," said one marine guard, who had let his hair and beard grow and was puffing on a pipeful of hashish. "Your boys kidnapped us, and now you're stuck with us!"

"You don't understand," Khomeini pleaded. "Last night your government tried sending a commando force in to grab you. It was just like in *Wee Wee Monsieur*, when the Stooges snuck into the Arab kingdom of Simmitz to free the captured soldier from the evil sheik! I don't want to be the evil sheik! *I want to be Moe*! If your American troops last night had filled up on gas before takeoff, they would have made it in here and—just like Stooges—found a damned harem!"

"Yikes!" A diplomat sat up on his waterbed. "If they ever broke in here and found us like this, we'd be finished!"

"I'll say," the marine nodded. "The corps would court-martial us!"

"To hell with the corps," the diplomat grunted. "The wives would kill us!"

There was silence in the room as the hostages considered this. Finally, one spoke from behind a Pac-man machine. "Ayatollah," he said, "I think you'd better split us up and move us to separate locations."

"No!" the ayatollah wailed. "I'm sending you all home!"

At once all fifty-two hostages began rolling on the floor, contorting their faces and moaning, "Ooooh! Torture, torture! They've whipped us and beat us! Oooh!"

"OK, OK," Khomeini spit. "You win. You can stay."

The hostages applauded.

"But this *can't* go on forever!"

"Booo."

Well, it didn't, of course. Those fifty-two pests wore out their welcome until the last possible minute, when the thought of new President Reagan, martyring them in a massive retaliation against Iran, sent them scurrying for their suitcases. I think it was Reagan's use of the term *prisoners of war* in referring to the fifty-two that really shook them. POWs, after all, are written off as military losses.

The ayatollah, grateful as he was that they were leaving,

hoped the hostages would at least not claim Iran had mistreated them.

"Don't you worry, Imam buddy," one shaggy GI said in parting. "I'll be just overjoyed to tell my wife and superiors all the belly-dancing fun we've been having for the last fourteen months."

Then, as the marine closed the door, he glanced back at Khomeini and, smiling, moaned, "Ooh. Torture! Beatings! Solitary confinement! Oooh." His giggle echoed down the hall.

"Well, Imam," I said to my red-faced boss, "at least they're finally gone."

"Don't kid yourself, Shemp," the weary ayatollah sighed, removing his black Moe Hair. "Americans always come back."

9
The Stooges as Propagandists in World War II

"Do you want us to be patriotic and buy war bonds; or do you want us to be unpatriotic and pay the rent?"

Curly to Landlord, *Spook Louder* (1942)

OR AN ERA that has produced so much technology, fast food, and multisyllable words, the twentieth century has turned out rather few great philosophers. Yeah, there was Bertrand Russell sitting and accepting privileged guests into his parlor to watch him grouse; there was M. Ali discoursing on the inequities of race relations and the meaning of the heavyweight crown; there was Donovan. But for the most part, the alleged philosophers of our age were politicians or writers who used philosophy as an excuse for weak chops in their statecraft or prose. Usually a politico declares himself a philosopher about the time he picks up a gun and starts blasting away opponents on the old Catholic assumption that error had no rights. Mao would fit into this group. Sometimes politicians become philosophers about the time they themselves are staring down the rifle barrel (Trotsky's one of these). Most often, modern philosophers are unwanted fellows like Jean-Paul Sartre, declared a philosopher by writers and a writer by philosophers.

Why does our century suffer this void? Surely we've not lacked for great events to inspire deep thought. Perhaps it's the very enormality of those events that has struck philosophy mute. When faced with the horrors of Kampuchea or apartheid or nuclear weapons, intellectual discourses can seem almost in bad taste, a parlor game.

Active enthusiasts in WWII, the Three Stooges influenced the next generation of American leaders—from Viet Nam to Iran. History shows that General DeGaulle took his sense of humility from Moe, that General Patton (always an actor) took his sense of theatrics and face slapping from Larry, and that General Westmoreland grew up watching Curly destroy landscapes and demolish buildings.

Luckily for you, dear reader, taste has never been a criterion for this volume.

War with Germany

So let us examine how the great cauldron of the Second World War forged the philosophies of Curly, Moe, and Larry. Remember that, like many of their generation, the Stooges exhibited during the thirties pacifist—bordering on cowardly—inclinations. Yet while their contemporaries, Charles Lindbergh and Joseph Kennedy, were casting about for a way to reconcile isolationism with the growing evidence of Hitler's unprecedented rottenness, Howard, Fine, and Howard were

Photo courtesy Columbia Pictures Corporation.

demonstrating the sort of capacity for intellectual growth and moral courage that was to become their hallmark. The beach at Pearl Harbor had no sooner been swept than the Three Stooges were reevaluating their isolationist philosophies. By the time Paris was goose-stepping into 1942, the trio had thrown themselves into preparing their raging manifesto, *I'll Never Heil Again.* Perhaps, like LBJ watching Walter Cronkite denounce the war in Viet Nam, Hitler knew his cause was finished when the Three Stooges attacked him.

Certainly Adolph was hurt by Moe's portrayal of him. In this sweeping indictment, the Stooges are housepainters (Hitler's own summer job) pressed into leading a beer hall rebellion in the country of Moronika. When invited by the nation's foreign minister to become dictators, the boys ask for a job description. The minister explains that a dictator "makes love to beautiful women, drinks champagne, enjoys life, and never works. He makes speeches to the people promising them plenty, gives them nothing, and then takes everything."

"A parasite!" yelps Curly, tellingly invoking the Soviet label in allusion to the Stooges' socialist inclinations. "That's for me!"

Soon Moe is installed as dictator, Curly as field marshal, and Larry as minister of propaganda. Today's students too often forget that Nazism presented itself as a liberation from past oppression (much like today's "liberations" in Iran, Afghanistan, and, perhaps by the time this book sees print, Nicaragua). Moe alludes to this rationalization when he announces, "We must throw off the yoke of monarchy and make our country safe for hypocrisy!" Later Moe declares, "We want peace," to which his knowing minister responds, "Yes, a piece of this country and a piece of that."

Moe's Minister of Oompha warns him that minorities are creeping into the majorities, and Moe orders a man caught withholding a chicken from the dictator taken to "a concentrated camp."

Clearly the Stooges, pacifist though they might be, were riled by World War II into righteous fury. In this they were much like their great patron FDR, who also swung from socialist to militarist as the thirties emptied into the forties.

How ended the dictatorship of Moronika? In one of the most gruesome of Stoogely curtains, the corrupted Moe, Larry, and Curly are rent to ribbons by lions. Their flesh torn from their living bones, their screams producing no pity, the Dark Stooges die horribly. Sic semper tyrannis.

War with Japan

Real students of the Three Stooges take special delight in recalling the time Moe, Larry, and Curly were set on the trail of some Japanese-Americans who'd run off from the local relocation camp. Upon finding these unfortunates in an old barn, the Stooges tossed in sticks of dynamite and blew them all to oblivion.

Even now, it's hard to stifle a chuckle at the thought of how scared those nutty Nips looked just before the boys lit the fuse.

Which brings us to a discussion of the role the Stooges played in preparing America for the devastation of Hiroshima and Nagasaki by our forces in 1945. Perhaps Harry Truman, that beloved regular guy of a president, was concerned that some bleeding hearts wouldn't dig the notion of deep-frying whole cities when a nuked mountain or Pacific Island could make the point as clearly. Luckily, the Stooges made ready the way of the bomb way back in 1942, in the short they called *Spook Louder*. That epic must have been made with help from the Manhattan Project (either that or the Stooges thought the whole thing up on their own, and Oppenheimer and Teller took the ideas from them).

Either way, *Spook Louder* was a prescient piece of propaganda. The Stooges' sympathies are established early on, when Curly is asked, "You're not a Jap are you?" and responds by shouting, "Me? A Jap?!" and going for his accuser's throat.

Curly, Larry, and Moe are assigned to guard the inventions of a scientist named (note the symbolism) Doctor Graves. The scientist has been summoned off to the nation's capital to demonstrate his "new death ray machine." Graves can barely contain his joy as he brags, "It will destroy *millions*!" The Stooges are warned to protect all such inventions against Japanese spies.

"If enemy spies get fresh with us," Curly promises, his syntax choking on his own enthusiasm, "I'll dash their head against the wall, I'll rip off their arms, I'll break their eardrums!"

It is then that the scientist reveals to the Stooges (and the Stooges to the world) that he has a bomb that will "destroy anything and everything!" In an emergency, the Stooges are given permission to use it against the Japanese.

At this point the narrative moves into the symbolic with a power that makes *The Seventh Seal* look like "Bosom Buddies." Three spies do come looking for the secrets of the bomb—one dressed all in black (death), one dressed as Satan (evil), and one dressed as a skeleton (the victims). These three specters pursue the Stooges through the scientist's house, a house filled with ominously ticking clocks. Thus was introduced to the world the concept of the atomic clock, moving perilously close to midnight, and thus, when Moe, Larry, and Curly finally unleashed the bomb and destroyed their enemies, did our current age begin.

It would be three more years before the Stooges' grim vision would become reality, and it is yet debated whether they were prophets or inspiration for the real Doctor Graves who sent the cream pie of atomic destruction sailing into the faces of our own post-nuclear world.

One thing's for sure, though: those Japs certainly paid the price for crossing Curly and the boys.

A Little-known lyric found in the mattress of Oscar Hammerstein, Lorenzo Hart, or one of those guys:

Has anybody here seen my friend Moe Howard?
Can you tell me where he went?
He threw a lot of pies and he poked them in the eyes
And they stuck him in cement.
Anybody here seen my old friend Larry
With the violin and hair?
They called him Doctor Fine, and they called him porcupine
I don't see him anywhere.
Anybody here seen my old pal Curly?
Has he gone to Niagara Falls?
(At this, the singer pauses to survey the audience, who, in respectable theaters, can be expected to cry out in unison, "Niagara Falls!")
Whatever will we do without Woowoowoobuwoowoo
He's not on TV at all
   Didn't you love when Moe dressed like Hitler?
   Didn't you love when Larry showed his knobby knees
   And can-o-peas?
   Hey Moe, Hey Larry, Moe, Larry, the Cheese
Anybody here seen my old friend Shemp?
Was his hair slicked down with glue?
I saw him selling Brighto up over the hill
With Curly, Larry, and Moe
Hello, hello, hello

10
The Effect of the Stooges on U.S. Conduct in the Viet Nam War

IT'S HARD TO even think of the Viet Nam War without acknowledging the massive contributions of Curly, Larry, and Moe. The generations that fought the American Revolution, the Civil War, and the World Wars had all grown up thrilling to heroic tales of triumph in the face of grave odds and poems about victory snatched from the gaping maw of great adversity. But the little boys who would grow up to serve in Viet Nam were weaned on different war stories. Not for the '60s generation were the glories of *The Iliad* and "The Charge of the Light Brigade." No, the first TV generation grew up absorbing the Stooges notion of "All for one, one for all, and every man for himself!" The conscience-shaking attitudinal turnabout the Stooges advocated and achieved can best be illustrated in the famous scene when a general asks that one of the Three Soldiers volunteer to step forward for a dangerous mission. Larry and Moe each take a step back, leaving Curly the reluctant volunteer.

This made sense to the kids of the 60s. They looked at the War in Indochina, looked at the Stooges, looked at the War again and said, "Hell no, we won't go."

And in retrospect, they had the right idea. If every draftee had headed for the Canadian hills, America would have been spared a lot of grief. The real trouble wasn't with the stooges who refused to go to Viet Nam; the real trouble was with the stooges who went there—for the pervasive Stoogely influence spread to both sides of the fence.

One of the many peculiarities of the Viet Nam War was the phenomenon of "friendly fire," U.S. troops being bombarded by their own mixed-up comrades. Like so many of the idiosyncracies of that first war fought by the generation that grew up on the Stooges, the concept of friendly fire was of Stoogely origin.

In *Boobs in Arms*, Curly, Larry and Moe are trapped behind enemy lines, under attack when Moe cries out "Our own army is bombarding us!" Larry answers, "We'll get killed!" The next shot is of the Stooges being blown to heaven. There the story ends, a grim denouement, and one which made a great impression on the future draft dodgers of America.

How many times, in the reassessments, autopsies, and Monday morning quarterbacking that followed the defeat of the U.S. in Viet Nam, did we hear moaning professors maintain that we could have avoided that miserable little conflict if we as a nation had paid attention to the lessons of history. What a load of malarky. What could have kept our great ship of state from being beached on the sandbar of that Asian peninsula were the lessons of the Three Stooges! The lessons of history are what got us into the mess in the first place. The Stooges were among the few who realized from day one that Viet Nam was not a holy crusade like the Second World War. The Stooges' cowardly instincts warned them that Viet Nam was nothing but trouble. Too bad Lyndon Johnson wasn't as smart as Moe.

Some sub-intellectual readers may say, "Hold it here, prof. How can you paint Moe and the boys as Doves when we all know they approached the Second World War with gusto?" Sure, the Three Stooges had been gung ho about World War II! Who wouldn't be excited about a big war in which the bad guys were real, real bad, we got to keep the fighting three thousand miles from home, the locals wanted us there, and everybody else had been wearing themselves down for two or three years before we got there? World War II was a good one, as *Hogan's Heroes* and *McHale's Navy* make clear. But the trouble with wars is that everyone who grows up (let alone goes to a military academy) during one war then tries to apply that war's lessons to the next one.

But that's not the Stooges fault.

Larry, Moe, and Curly introduced an anti-war attitude into the best young minds of the generation that would grow up to shout "No way!" when Uncle Sam beckoned. In *Dizzy Pilots* the Stooges desperately tried to design a new airplane so that they could avoid the draft. (They called it "The Buzzard." Howard Hughes obviously patterned his own "Spruce Goose" after this Moe-ish innovation.) It was made quite clear throughout the adventure that the Stooges did not care one whit if their airplane would perform or not; they only cared about staying out of the war. How many students of the 60s viewed their college education the same way?

The Stooges always considered military conscription with disgust. In *Wee Wee Monsieur* they race from the draft board, only to have bars drop in front of the door. The Berrigan Brothers 1960s trashings of Selective Service headquarters were as much tributes to the Howard Brothers as acts of guerilla resistance.

Some of the Stooges other innovations were imitated by the young recruits who were sent to Viet Nam. In *Boobs in Arms* the boys were G.I.s whose evil sergeant declared, "I'm going to make soldiers out of you guys if it KILLS you—and I hope I do!" How like the mindset that would, in southeast Asia explain, "We had to destroy that village in order to save it!"

Years later *M*A*S*H* would get lots of credit for lampooning the militarist mentality. But Hawkeye's barbs were gentle indeed when compared to the vengeful satire of the Stooges. In *Boobs in Arms* the commander is a cruel, low IQ bully who tries to impale the boys on his bayonet. The Stooges' retaliation is to try to finish him off on the battlefield. In Viet Nam this sort of tomfoolery would be nicknamed "fragging."

Later on, Curly is about to be stabbed by the enemy when he throws the Sergeant between himself and the sword. Unfortunately this innovative defense is interrupted by a gas attack from the Stooges own forces.

During the actual Viet Nam war, Moe and Larry maintained an official silence on the subject, much like those kept by Bob

Dylan and (until just before his death) Martin Luther King, Jr. No doubt if Moe had lent his support to the U.S. policies, the generation that he stepfathered would have thrown down their peace signs and marched off to Indochina. But Moe withstood the pressure and held his tongue. There was no need for the Stooge to speak out against the war in Viet Nam. His work was eloquent enough.

11
The Effect of the Stooges on Social Etiquette

MANNERS, AS MUCH as the opposable thumb, are what separate the humans from the lower primates. Monkeys may enjoy social relationships, the range of emotions, and a crimson sunset as much as we do, but monkeys do not know which fork to use on a lobster tail.

Manners are the key to social acceptability, the last bastion of the class system. In this democratic society, a man may buy his way into the best organizations; a poor but industrious lad may get into Princeton on scholarship alone. But manners are the sure brand of breeding.

Which is why those uncertain of their social status get so nervous when confronted with questions of etiquette. Dunk your corn in the fingerbowl just once, and four years of college go out the window.

The Three Stooges, who had no doubts about their own class or merit, took great amusement from the efforts of the less cultured to barnstorm their way into the stratosphere of polite society. "Where's your Emily Post?" Moe demanded, and social divas shrank into the woodwork in mortification.

Dear Emily Post,
What is the correct method for determining the proper temperature at which to serve white wine at a formal banquet?

J. Onassis

Dear J.O.,
According to *An Ache in Every Stake*, the correct method is
to produce a thermometer from one's pocket and stick it in
one's neighbor's beverage. If the drink is determined to be too
warm, one should signal the server to produce a small ice
cube on a long pair of tongs and use the tongs to drop ice
into the glass.

E.P.

The Stooges had no use for the social aspirations so often
tied to etiquette. For them manners were a mark of refine-
ment, not a shortcut to achieving it. Given the chance, Curly
and the boys would upend the pretensions of the desperate
elite with a glee usually associated with small boys pulling the
wings from flies. In *Slippery Silks*, the Stooges pass themselves off as French fashion designers and humiliate a society
matron anxious to be the first with the latest.

In *Tassels in the Air*, a noveau riche woman wants to have
her home redesigned by the hottest decorator in town—not
because the house needs it but because she wants to show up
a friend who admires the decorator. Keeping up with the
Rockefellers is everything in this sad social stratum; the wife
tells her husband that with the proper decorator they could
get into *Who's Who* and perhaps even the golf club. Needless to
say, the Stooges, now appearing as interior decorators, scotch
her ambitions and destroy her chances of teeing off.

Dear Emily Post,
What etiquette should be observed by partners at cards when
teamed against strangers?

P. Caroline of Monaco

Dear P.C. of M.,
According to *Goofs and Saddles*, one player should exclaim to
his partner, "I have four kinks in my back." The partner
should respond by slipping off his shoe and counting his
ally's toes in order to determine an advantageous bid.

E.P.

Never did the Stooges tear into the insecurities of social climbers with more verve than in *Termites of 1938*, when they sat down at a grand dinner and began stuffing their napkins in their collars. At once the uneasy guests followed suit, no one secure enough to sway from the herd. Soon the boys were piling their potatoes on their knives and popping peas into their mouths while the whole banquet did likewise. Has the peer pressure and lack of social grace of the would-be upper class ever been more devastatingly lampooned? Not since Oscar Wilde, anyway. Of course, the biggest laugh of all is that a couple of the Stooges' alleged dining room malapropisms— like eating chicken with the fingers—have been accepted as proper in even the stuffiest society. And at least one shot—of an elegant table prepared with the knives and forks on the same side of the plates—suggests that Moe and the boys may have been a little socially unsteady in real life, as well as on camera.

Dear Emily Post,
What is the proper method of addressing a policeman?

J. Delorean

Dear J.D.
According to *Mutts to You,* one should slap the officer and say, "Oh, a cop, eh? Always pushin' people. I've always wanted to punch a cop right in the nose." Then exit.

E.P.

Before John Paul were Paul and John. Before Curly Joe were Joe and Curly. The implications could shatter world views.

12
The Influence of the Three Stooges on the Modern Papacy

THE ROMAN CATHOLIC Church had survived from the time of the apostles until the 1950s with its sense of order and propriety intact. The Church had run into threats from outside (the Roman persecution, the Protestant Reformation) and from inside (selling indulgences, Spanish Inquisiting) without ever losing the pizzazz that made this Church the only Church that ever got to be *the* Church.

But by the late 1950s, Catholicism was faced with a world that seemed to be moving away from the religious impulse toward a secular morality. When Pope Pius XII died, a long string of Piuses was broken, and the Church found herself faced with the task of finding a pope who could speak to a world familiar with the Three Stooges.

It was no easy task, for while regal princes, dour ascetics, and authoritative saints were good enough for the world gone by, the cardinals who met in Rome to choose Pius's successor knew that the global popularity of Moe, Larry, and Curly set a new standard that Rome would have to match or else see Mother Church lose more ground to humanism and other worldly rivals. Meeting in conclave, the princes of the Church waited for inspiration from the Holy Ghost and tried to imagine how Del Lord would handle the choices before them.

Although recounting the details of what goes on in a papal conclave is punishable by excommunication, this has not

stopped the great cleric/theological scholar/romance novel-
ists of our time from reconstructing ballot-by-ballot descrip-
tions of how popes are chosen. Using the same tools as these
scholars (unnamed sources, gifts of the Paraclete), we can
easily reconstruct the debate that went on within these closed
councils over which of the Stooges should be the model for the
first post-Stoogely pontiff.

Larry, long-suffering and self-chastising, would have been
the choice of the Franciscans and all those unrepresented
nuns and monks in the nunneries and monkeries of the globe.
Those who suffer in silence would have looked to Larry as role
model and considered that the grief he accumulated, properly
offered up, could free legions from Purgatory.

Certainly Larry's willingness to haul himself around by his
own earlobe, to yank out great hunks of his own hair, to knock
himself on the forehead with his own fist, was in direct line
with the ancient tradition of self-flagellation and mortification of the flesh. Larry's use of the expression "Ah kid'ya not"
may or may not have been his own voicing of the medieval
prohibition against acedia—the sin of *enjoying* self-flagelat-
ing and flesh mortifying.

The humble monks who would have prayed most fervently
for the ascension of a Larry to the Throne of St. Peter would
also have appreciated nature's gift to Larry of a monk's
tonsure, the small shaved patch in the hair at the crown of the
skull. Not stigmata, perhaps, but saints have been canonized
on lesser proofs.

Still, the papal conclave ultimately dismissed the notion of a
Larry-like pope, for the same reason they always dismiss the
choices of the humble and long-suffering—the humble and
long-suffering don't know how to handle a floor fight.

Moe, on the other hand, was the role model favored by the
Curia, the Vatican-based cardinals who run the Church's
more Machiavellian and business-like practices. The Doctrine
of Infallibility, invoked only twice in the history of the Church,
was invoked by Moe about sixty times a day. Much misunder-
stood in the non-Catholic world, the Doctrine of Papal Infallibility does not assert that the pope knows who's going to win
the World Series. Rather, it invests in the pope an authority

much like that which the American Constitution invests in the U.S. Supreme Court. Infallibility means that when the pope speaks *ex cathedra* the argument is over—the case is closed.

Many conservative cardinals wouldn't have minded a pope who would speak *ex cathedra* a little more often—and that was the appeal of a Moe-pope, one who would rule with an iron fist, a firm voice, and unwavering faith in his own infallibility.

The conclave argued on and on. What sort of pope could stem the tide of secularism, of materialism, of sensualism? The Catholic and non-Catholic worlds were no longer isolated from each other. The next pope's would have to be a voice that Catholics would follow and non-Catholics would respect and understand. Clearly what was needed was a voice that went "Nyuk nyuk nyuk."

In choosing a Curly, the cardinals voted to turn toward a church of joy. Pope John XXIII was jolly like Curly, fat like Curly, bald like Curly. As a PR move in a world still reeling from the death of Curly and the death of one pope, the emergence of John seemed like a recombinant resurrection; it was as if Curly had returned from heaven with the Keys to the Kingdom dangling from his fob.

What many cardinals did not expect was that Pope John's debt to Curly went beyond the obvious, outward influences. Pope John's actions echoed Curly's own. In *Disorder in the Court,* Curly had admonished the bailiff to "Stop talkin' pig Latin!" With the Second Vatican Council, Pope John carried that admonition to the whole Catholic world. The universal Latin mass was translated into the vernacular ("That ain't a vernacular," John was once heard to admonish; "that's a miter.") with all the enthusiasm of the Stooges dismantling a posh party. Pope John tore through the traditions of the Church with the same destructive gusto that Curly brought to staid colleges, military standards, and upper-crust orthodoxy. Every time the Stooges were given authority—made professors or opera singers or interior decorators—they set about destroying the conventions around them. So did John XXIII go after the dogmas of Catholicism, from Mariology to fish on Friday.

But like Curly, John XXIII's flame glowed so brightly that it burned out quickly. Soon the Curly pope was dead, and the cardinals had to choose a successor. Luckily, they had the example of Moe and Larry to look to for guidance. Moe and Larry had replaced Curly not with a Curly clone, but with an ally as dour as Curly was cheerful, as thin and ascetic as Curly was rotund and boisterous. As the Stooges chose Shemp, so the cardinals chose Giovanni Battista Montini, Pope Paul VI.

How alike they were! Both sad men, men of great talent, laboring in the shadow of a brilliant and beloved predecessor. And with unreasonable harshness did the world study them, dismiss them, blame them for not being as inspired as the men they succeeded.

In all the world, perhaps only Lyndon Johnson could truly understand how lonely a place Shemp and Paul VI occupied.

Dutifully, Shemp took the slaps, the eye pokes, the insults. Yet he knew he was only taking part in a reenactment of the chaos Curly had created in inspired freedom. So too was Paul left to ratify all of John's revolutions. He was figuratively poked in the eyes and spiritually slapped in the chops.

By the time Paul VI passed on, it was clear to the Church what the passing of Shemp had made clear to the Stooges: better to have an imitation Curly than an original anybody else.

So the Stooges went to Joe DeRita and then quickly to Joe Besser. And they called him "Curly Joe," combining the names of his predecessors. The princes of the Catholic Church again took their cue from the Stooges. They went to Albino Luciani, and then quickly to Karol Wojtyla. And they called him "John Paul," combining the names of *his* predecessors.

"Be round and jolly like the first guy," they admonished. "Maybe from a distance nobody will know the difference."

13
The Influence of the Stooges on American Jurisprudence

THESE COURT TRANSCRIPTS *came into possession of the American Stooge Symposium after one of our members, J. Edward "Rocky" Kelleher, was possessed at a seance by the spirit of Oliver Wendell Holmes. Speaking through Kelleher, Justice Holmes recounted how a court was convened in the Next World to determine whether the United States should be destroyed for sins against the Divine Spirit of the Law. It seems that Justice herself was weighing the scales against America, when Three Powerful Spirits came to the nation's aid. What follows is a rare insight into judicial proceedings in the hereafter.*

COTTON MATHER: Hear ye, hear ye! The Eternal Court of the Swift Sword of Divine Retribution and Final Judgment is called to order! Repent all ye sinners lest ye be cast into fiery Perdition! The righteous judge Solomon presides! All rise!

SOLOMON: Be seated! What petition is brought before this court?

COTTON MATHER: Your honor! We have heard the prayers of the ayatollahs, the medicine men, and TV evangelists that the corrupt and sinful United States of America be smitten from the earth!

SOLOMON: Who represents the petitioners?

DRACO: I, Solomon, Draco of Greece, shall prove to the court that this corrupt nation merits no mercy but deserves the contempt of heaven! *(Cheers from assembled demons and the souls of the damned.)*

SOLOMON: And who speaks in the defense of the United States?

WEBSTER: I, your honor, Daniel Webster of New Hampshire. The United States may have her legalistic faults, but also hers are virtues to light the paths of justice through the darkest nights of her despair. Turn away from these baseless libels and dismiss the groundless accusations of those heathens whose pleas dishonor this Hereafter. *(Cheers from Seraphim and Cherubim.)*

DRACO: Objection, your honor. Counsel seeks to prejudice jury against heathens.

SOLOMON: Sustained. Jurors will ignore Mister Webster's aspersion. Reverend Mather? Where did you find this jury?

COTTON MATHER: The jurors, your grace, are the Great Executed: The fellow with the ostrich neck is Nathan Hale, the gentleman seated upside down is Saint Peter, the woman with the toast is Joan of Arc, and the fellow with the six-pack of Pepto is Socrates. The couple on the end with the lampposts up their backs are the Mussolinis. Seated in the second row are Julius Caesar, Thomas Beckett, General Custer, Marie Antoinette, Gary Gilmore, and Anne Boleyn.

SOLOMON: Well, that's what I call a hung jury. Prosecutor, present your evidence.

DRACO: The case makes itself, honored Solomon. The United States was once a nation dedicated to stern justice and swift retribution. As such it was favored by Heaven and stood blessed among the kingdoms of the earth. But in recent years the nation's sense of justice has decayed until it has become a mockery. Innocent men fester in cells while criminals walk the streets with impunity. Judges change their opinions with the political winds and contradict each other with no thought to consistency.

WEBSTER: Solomon, if these are capital sins, man stood condemned before Pharoah judged Moses.

DRACO: This is merely the background, your honor, against which the U.S.A.'s current crimes are committed. Here are the specifics: First, the U.S. Supreme Court made its Miranda decision, declaring it the obligation of the constabulary to protect the rights of the accused, even to inform them of those rights before arresting them. Clearly a mockery of justice as we recognize her. In the years that followed; the abuses became more flagrant. We have recently seen an assassin in San Francisco defended on the basis that the junk food he ate made him guiltless of his crimes; the accused Von Bulow's conviction was overturned on a technicality, only to have the second judge disallow all the prosecution's best evidence for fear of a similar overturning; nuisance suits are allowed the full respect and sympathy of the law, with judges regularly doling out huge awards to alleged victims of accidents once rightly recognized as acts of God; in Florida a man was allowed to excuse his murdering on the grounds that he watched too much violent television. Finally, a would-be assassin shot the president of the United States in the chest and was found not guilty by reason of insanity. All these travesties together, your honor, demonstrate beyond any doubt that the United States is a just nation no longer. To allow her to continue is to extend to Dame Justice the middle finger of impunity.

SOLOMON: Boy, I'll say. I guess we'll all be out of here before lunch.

WEBSTER: Perhaps not, your honor. Defense must ask the jury to recognize that all these excesses are born of a desire to be scrupulous in protecting the rights of men. All are based on the premise that it is better that ten guilty men go free than one innocent be punished unjustly!

MARIE ANTOINETTE: Yeah, sure!

NATHAN HALE: Easy for you to say!

DRACO: Honored King Solomon. Can't we just wrap this up now?

SOLOMON: I don't see why not. Webster? Ready to throw in the towel?

WEBSTER: A moment's indulgence, your honor. Ladies and gentlemen of the jury, would you respect the voice of Thomas Jefferson?

JURY: Boo! Jerk!

WEBSTER: Abraham Lincoln?

JURY: Phawww! Hang 'em all!

WEBSTER: The Three Stooges?

JURY: The Three Stooges? I love the Stooges! Not Joe Besser, right? The real Curly? Oh boy!

DRACO: Solomon, I object! The Three Stooges are still pending canonization. It is entirely unclear whether they are fit to testify.

SOLOMON: The bench must agree, Mister Webster. Much as we would all like to meet the Stooges, on what grounds can we accept their testimony as expert in a divine judicial proceeding?

WEBSTER: Your honor, prosecution's contention is based on the premise that American justice has decayed since the Miranda decision in the late sixties. I believe that the Stooges can prove that every single one of the recent cases Draco cited has precedent years earlier—in the decades the court recognizes as a period when the United States was a blessed nation!

SOLOMON: OK by me. Draco?

DRACO: Very well, your honor. But I hope Mister Webster bears in mind that any attempt to turn this court into a circus could be judged blasphemy and result in my colleague and his witnesses being cast into hell. *(Cheers from demons.)*

CURLY'S VOICE *(Outside the courtoom)*: Hell! Nya ah ah!

SOLOMON: Enter the Three Stooges!

MOE: Hello!

LARRY: Hello!

CURLY: Hello!

STOOGES: Hello!

SOLOMON: *Sit down!*

WEBSTER: Gentlemen, do you not all hail from the twentieth-century United States?

CURLY: Soitainly!

WEBSTER: And did you not all have experience with the legal proceedings of that nation in the 1930s and 1940s?

MOE: Wait a minute, pal. I can explain. Like we told the angel out front when we got here, we never meant to do nothin' wrong. There was extenuatin' soicumstances! Like that bit with the stolen car. We thought . . .

WEBSTER: Mister Howard, you are not on trial here. Your place in Heaven is secure. We are merely seeking your insights into the state of the American judicial system in the days before the 1950s. For example, in the 1980s a killer's violence was excused on the grounds that he ate too much junk food. Do you recall any precedent for such a contention? Take your time.

LARRY: Why yeah! That's like the way Curly used to go nuts whenever he'd hear *Pop Goes the Weasel* or see a tassel!

WEBSTER: I see. And how would you calm this raging bull?

CURLY: That's easy! They'd feed me some cheese!

WEBSTER: I see. So in your experience, gentlemen, there was some relation between violent acts and nutrition.

MOE: You said it! Why once these mugs dropped a flapjack on my face, and I beat them to *(sees Solomon glaring)*, uh, that is, I turned the other cheek and forgave them. *(Astonished looks from Larry and Curly.)*

WEBSTER: But what of courts that protect the rights of criminals? Surely these did not exist under the swift sword of the 1930s?

CURLY: Are you kiddin? Why, some of them judges was real softies. Take his honor in *A Plumbin' We Will Go*: he took one look at us, got all sentimental, and started bawlin' out the cop who brought us in. He says, "Mister Prosecutor, you have not proved that these men were actually in that chicken coop. Your evidence is purely circumstantial and insufficient to warrant a conviction. And in the future, Officer Kelly, don't come cluttering up this courtroom with flimsy charges against law-abiding citizens! Case dismissed!"

WEBSTER: Sounds very cut and dried. And then what happened?

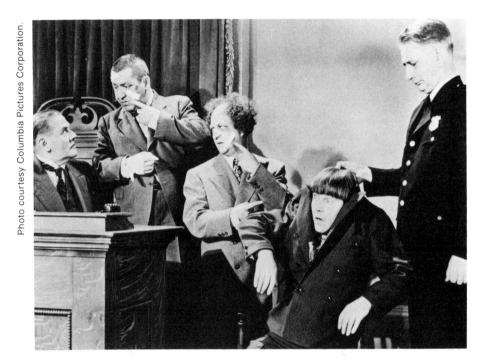

Photo courtesy Columbia Pictures Corporation.

CURLY: Why, I went to put on my hat, and all them chicken feathers fell out!

WEBSTER: I see. Now, in recent years the United States has been criticized for using technicalities to disallow evidence in criminal proceedings. I don't suppose that ever happened in the good old days, did it?

MOE: What are you, nuts? Didn't you ever see our picture, *Disorder in the Court*? That judge ruled all the testimony out of order! Why, even when we started wreckin' the place he just rapped his gavel and said, "Gentlemen, you must control your killing instincts!"

DRACO: All right, all right! The prosecution will concede that there have always been soft judges! But what of the other travesties against justice we have cited? What about the rash of nuisance suits that have made the American courtroom a substitute for the back alley brawl?

Webster: Well, gentlemen? What about it?

Moe: Well, your highness, I wouldn't want to say too much about whatever little pranks my pals and I might've pulled in our younger days. . . .

Solomon: *Answer the question or suffer eternal torment!*

Curly: Woowoowoowoowoo!

Larry: Well, judge, it's like this. One time—*Loco Boy Makes Good*—Moe read in the paper that a man collected thirty thousand dollars in damages from a hotel when he slipped on a cake of soap in the lobby.

Webster: And how did Moe act on this information?

Larry: Why, he bought some soap!

Webster: And then?

Curly: He brought us to a hotel and said, "You start slippin' and we start suin'!"

Moe *(to Curly)*: Remind me to kill you later.

Curly: You can't! I'm already dead! Nyuk nyuk nyuk. *(Moe pokes Curly in eyes.)*

Draco: Say! Leave him alone!

Webster: Ah, shaddup.

Draco: What! Why you provincial . . .take this! *(Hits Webster. Demons cheer. Cherubim shoot tiny arrows at demons, who howl and expectorate at angels.)*

Solomon: Order in the court! Order! *(Thunder rips through courtroom. All quiet down.)*

WEBSTER: Forgive me, your eminence. I wanted to demonstrate to the court how watching violence—like the Three Stooges—could indeed lead to violent behavior. I trust my point is well made? Unless esteemed Draco wishes to contend that he and the other souls attendant are more susceptible to sinful influence than are the people of America?

SOLOMON: Draco?

DRACO: Prosecution concedes that the Three Stooges have a special gift for inspiring mayhem in even the gentlest of hearts. But, your honor, there is still one charge these witnesses have not answered, one charge that by itself will condemn the United States of America to the fate of Sodom and Gomorrah. There is no precedent for this ludicrous "insanity defense" that excuses the worst sort of violence and mayhem on the self-evident grounds that the perpetrator is nuts! Find that in your experience, Misters Howard, Fine, and Howard!

CURLY: Say, he reminds me of that rat Fleecem, who got me socked with alimony for usin' bad words!

WEBSTER: Well, gentlemen? What about it? Does the insanity defense ring a bell? I don't suppose anything like that could have been used in a court of law in the old days, eh?

LARRY: Why, you . . . don't remind me . . .

CURLY: Arf! Arf!

MOE: Shaddup, the both o' yas. You deserved it!

WEBSTER: Deserved what? Gentlemen, tell the court what dark memory these questions has illuminated.

CURLY: Well, judge, it was like this: *Babes in the Woods*, I think it was . . .

LARRY: The worst of it was I had to live through it three times—once with me and Curly gettin' it, once with me and Shemp, and finally with me and Joe. And each was worse than the one before it!

WEBSTER: Each what?

LARRY: Each beatin' Moe gave us! We were shot, burned, beaten, and bit by bears!

WEBSTER: My goodness, and Moe just stood by?

CURLY: Moe did it! He moidered us!

MOE: Next time, remind me to do it poimanent!

WEBSTER: I see. And did this case come to court?

CURLY: Soitainly! In the thirties, the forties, and the fifties!

WEBSTER: And what did the courts of the United States in those hard, just righteous times rule?

MOE: That they deserved it!

WEBSTER: Why, sir?

MOE: Because they drove me nuts! *(Angels, demons, and jurors talk excitedly.)*

SOLOMON: Order! Order! Draco, it seems to this court that every charge you allege represents a recent decay in the judicial tradition of the United States has been shown to have precedents dating back decades. We cannot find it in our hearts to condemn that nation now when in the past we have blessed it. Have you anything to say?

DRACO: Yeah, *(eyeing Stooges hatefully)*, lemme at 'em! I'll moider the bums!

STOOGES: Nya ah ah!

(Courtroom dissolves into chaos, as Draco, the demons, and half the jury tear after the Stooges, who flee on the backs of nubile angel babes, lightning bolts blasting their butts.)

He got the external affectations right, but Pablo couldn't match Curly's buoyant spirit. Photo courtesy Wide World photos.

14
The Effect of the Stooges on Twentieth-Century Art

I N THE 1960s Andy Warhol and his peers in the pop movement made a big media bang by blowing up the advertising and other mundane artifacts of the era into paintings. This was art—or at least art world commodity—and this was started by the Three Stooges in the 1930s. Serious artists—if not art students and critics—know that pop art was created in 1942's *Matri Phony*, when Moe and Larry as painters made a canvas of a tic-tac-toe game. Right there the Stooges asserted in one bold stroke (well, four bold strokes) the soon-to-be favored notion that art is defined by the context in which the work is received. In other words, stuff your dead dog and he's just a dead stuffed dog. But sit that stuffed dog on a pedestal and he's *art*. It's the eye of the beholder; it's the thinking that makes it so.

The Stooges set the standard—and often painted the prototype—for almost all of what's modern in fine art. Roy Lichtenstein made art of comic book panels. Christo, with his "Running Fence" and other pieces of "environmental art" made art of nature. All very nice but nothing close to what the Three Stooges achieved a generation earlier when they made comic books of *themselves*. Next to that transmogrification the efforts of Cristo seem overreaching and clumsy, Lichtenstein insignificant.

In 1935's *Pop Goes the Easel* (even the name was prophetic), Moe took a bucket of paint, hurled it against a

Mr. Howard's "Three Musicians": Inspiration. Photo courtesy Columbia Pictures Corporation.

canvas, and announced his new work complete. Jackson Pollack spent his lifetime trying to capture the transcendence of that single moment.

But where did Moe, Larry, and Curly's gifts come from, and why has the art world refused them the credit they so richly deserve? Well, the art world, as parochial and inbred as any hamlet in Iceland, can forgive any indiscretion except a life that recognizes pursuits other than art. The Stooges were renaissance men, devoting as much energy to their music, philosophy, and flying-machine-building as to their painting. This diversity put them, as men and as spirits, in the class of

F. Leger's "Three Musicians": Artiface. Photo courtesy Museum of Modern Art, New York.

Leonardo. But it won them the jealousy of a pinched and territorial clique.

Not that the Stooges cared! They were creators of the first order, content to prepare the feast and let posterity gather the table scraps. (Graffiti art may be a *cause celebre* in SoHo, but it was a passing whim to those three celebrants of public defacing.)

Not that Curly and company were without inspirations of their own. Their eyes gleamed with the same mad twinkle that illuminated Van Gogh's, and they paid Vincent tribute each time Moe threatened to tear Larry's ear off.

Pablo Picasso said it took him a lifetime of experience to learn to paint like a child. Some people are just slow learners. The Stooges wasted much less time than P.P. in reverting to fingerpainting level, and so accomplished more in a rather limited career as fine artists than the Grand Old Man did in an extended lifetime of frantic busywork. Pablo, a contemporary of the Howards, affected a Curly haircut and girth only after the 3S. began climbing to fame on the underground bohemian vaudeville circuit. Many of the women portrayed in Picasso's paintings bear obvious similiarities to the Rubenesquely proportioned babes who inevitably chased Curly through the Stooges' two-reelers, and a tremendous amount of the rendering that was labeled "abstract" by the spatially retarded critics of the day is nothing more than Picasso's *literal* portrayal of men and women with their tonsils torn out, brains bashed in, and other attributes envisioned and described (but not put to canvas) by Moe.

Pablo Picasso—great twentieth-century painter—simply made a career out of committing to oil the ideas that the Three Stooges cast off in casual conversation. In this, Picasso was really more an illustrator than a true artist. Certainly *Guernica*, once taken by naive design school freshmen to be a significant comment on the Spanish Civil War, is nothing more than a rather mundane delineation of several of Moe's more gruesome threats.

In *suggestion*, these ideas had power and the clarity of the specific imagination. Giving them material form emasculated the imagination of the participant, substituting in its place a pedestrian—and rather unattractive—physical rendering of an idea that in its pure, Moeish form had the strength of infinite possibilities. One can look at the painting *Guernica* and shrug, "Looks like Dracula's wallpaper." How much more resonant are Moe's ten words, "Blow out the candle or I'll blow out your brain." Do we have to *see* the candle? Do we have to *see* the blown-out brain? One of Moe's words was worth a thousand of Picasso's pictures. Moe would say, "knuckle-head," and a thousand minds would conjure a thousand different images. Picasso had to draw a head full of knuckles.

Had he hung on into the 1980s, Pablo P. would undoubtedly have gone to work for MTV, making videos to take the imagination out of songs.

Posterity took its revenge on charlatans when the New York Museum of Modern Art finally shipped *Guernica* back to Spain, even as the Museum of Broadcasting across Fifth Avenue drew long lines to study the Stooges.

A painter with a less loathsome connection to the Stooges is the American Edward Hopper, who based most of his work on the backgrounds used in the Stooges' shorts. The Depression era American streets and rural landscapes of Hopper's work always seem to be just one frame to the left of Curly, Larry, and Moe, suitcases in hand and thumbs extended. Hopper's characters tended toward a solid stockiness much like Curly's own, and his empty Main Streets and dingy diners suggested a Super Service Station around each corner and a bottle of Bright-O under every counter.

Too bad that in his lifetime Hopper didn't get an eighth of the homage paid to that Stooge-copier, Picasso. The more one thinks about the injustice of it, the angrier one becomes! I mean, Pablo *I'm-so-cool* Picasso! Let's have *Life* magazine come down and take pictures of us playing nude Ping-Pong with our kids! Oh, that's OK—I'm *Pablo Picasso*. I'm Mister Artsy Fartsy. But let Moe tweak Larry's nose, and the Mutant Mothers of Middle America want the Stooges yanked off the local cable station because they're a bad influence on children! It's a goddamned national disgrace, is what it is!

Do you know how cheap Picasso was? When he ate in a restaurant, he wouldn't leave the waitress a tip. Instead, he'd yank out a Crayola and sketch a crude daisy on a napkin and tell her it would be worth a fortune someday because he was *Pablo Genius Picasso*. The waitress should have remembered the scene from *Wee Wee Monsieur* when Curly, as a Parisian painter, offers to pay his landlord the rent with his new masterpiece, the surrealistic *Maid on a Night out Winding a Grandfather's Clock with Her Left Hand*. The landlord says phooey, and Curly (obviously taking a big dig at Picasso) says, "What do you mean, 'phooey'? This'll be worth a fortune when I'm dead!" Replies the landlord, "I should kill you now and find out!"

But what of Curly's painting itself? What of his *Maid on a Night out* . . . While the digs at Picasso are obvious (Pablo probably swiped from the painting, looking for inspiration in another's send-up of him), the more startling revelation is that Curly's canvas, with its suspended ovals and disciplined surrealism, shows how great was the Stooge's influence on Salvador Dali, who captured one essence of Moe, Larry, and Curly that forever eluded Pablo "Macho Man" Picasso—a sense of humor.

And Dali's best stuff does have a certain Stoogely resonance; it does plant the ludicrous amid the conventions of the stately with a slapdash joy that would do the Stooges proud. Sal Dali snuck the little nutty twist into the perfectly appointed landscape in much the manner of Larry eating the peas with his knife at a formal banquet.

Unfortunately, Dali was so enamored of the Stooges that his life outside the studio took on a rather desperately slapstick air. It's never wise for the student to put on the master's mortarboard, and Dali's attempts to disrupt society with the spastic grace of Moe and the boys often came across as heavy-handed and obvious. Dali defecated in a dresser drawer in order to shock his mother when she opened it. How sad. He wanted so much to be the fourth Strooge, but his imagination wasn't up to the assignment. Would Curly have crapped in a bureau? Certainly not. He had just a little more élan than that. Curly would have carefully unhinged the whole room so that when Mom pulled open the drawer the wall collapsed and revealed the man next door sitting in the bathtub.

Although it is not known if young Sally Dali ever went to Hollywood to pay homage to his mentors, it seems likely the Stooges were aware of him. In *Pop Goes the Easel*, a painter bearing a remarkable likeness to Sal tries desperately to blot out the sun. An almost classical example of the artist striving for the unattainable, it is perhaps a subtle, knowing comment from Howard, Fine, and Howard on the attempts of young Dali to fly as close to the sun as his inspirations.

We cannot condemn Dali for failing to attain true Stoogeliness, though. His heart was in the right place even if his turd was not. Were we to judge as a failure every man who is unable to equal the artistic accomplishments of Larry, Moe, and Curly, we would be forced to condemn the whole of humanity.

After this historic, heretofore undisclosed luncheon, public morality was never the same. (left to right: G. G. Liddy, C. Q. Howard, L. Fine, J. E. Hoover, H. R. Haldeman, J. DeLorean.)

15
The Effect of the Stooges on Watergate

IN 1974, SHORTLY before Moe Howard died, he was reached by telephone by a disc jockey on radio station WBRU in Providence. The deejay asked Moe if, given the Stooges' own dubious on-screen morality, he thought their actions might have had some influence on the Watergate felons.

"What?!" Moe responded with the vengeful vigor he used to reserve for Curly after getting a faceful of ink. "We had nothin' to do with those jerks!"

Well, maybe not directly, Doctor Howard, but your influence surely shaped those young minds that grew up to deface the nation. Could anyone look at H. R. Haldeman, Richard Nixon's chief hatchet man, and not see in his eyes the glare of Moe on a bad day? Who could miss the connection between Chuck Colson's sudden interest in the Lord as he approached the witness stand and the Stooges' own tendency, when under extreme stress, to break into shouts of "Hallelujah, brothers!"

And what else are we to make of G. Gordon Liddy? Much has been written about Liddy's childhood fascination with the radio speeches of Adolph Hitler, but where do you think young Gordo spent his Saturday afternoons? Based on his future behavior, would it not be safe to assume little Liddy took in a few Stooges shorts down at the old movie parlor?

Look at the evidence: here's a guy who led a band of screwed-up, would-be burglars who called themselves *the Plumbers*.

Photo courtesy Columbia Pictures Industries, Inc., copyright 1975.

Any similarities are purely coincidental, right?

Photo courtesy Columbia Pictures Corporation.

Photo courtesy Columbia Pictures Corporation.

Photo courtesy Wide World photos.

Plumbers! The most Stoogely of professions, the career in which Moe, Larry, and Curly wreaked their greatest havoc. Liddy and his pal Howard Hunt didn't call their band the Howling Commandos or UNCLE; they baptised it in reverence for a reference to the Three Stooges.

And who was ever more Stoogelike in the execution of their duties? They taped the lock open the wrong way so that the tape came around the front of the door and was visible to the night watchman. And when said night watchman ripped that tape off and then went on his way, did they thank heaven for not being caught? No, in true Curly fashion they went back and *taped the door the wrong way again*!

When captured, the Watergaters behaved with all the fortitude of the Stooges under torture—they started throwing each other to the lions. Watching the behavior of the Watergate Stooges from the lowest burglar on up into the White House itself brought to mind that old Stooge motto: "All for one! One for all! Every man for himself!"

Throughout the sordid Watergate revelations, one was reminded of Moe's words: "Five hundred dollars! Who do we have to moider?"

Where did this contempt for the law begin? It seems to have had its roots in the Stooges' own remarks about their childhood. "My father died dancing," Curly gaily remarked to one woman he was waltzing around the dance floor. "At the end of a rope."

How could the impressionable young boys who would become the backbone of the Nixon administration fail to be impressed by such dashing disregard for the constraints of straight society? And young Gordon Liddy was the most impressionable of all. Only a true Stooge would climb a tree in a thunderstorm, as Liddy bragged of doing. Most of all, only a spiritual son of Curly would eat a rat. ("See this buttonhole?")

Curly, Larry, and Moe never missed a shot at a good swindle, and neither did Spiro Agnew—but even more than ethics, Agnew took from Curly a deftness in athletics that repeatedly found the vice president serving tennis balls into the back of his teammates' heads.

Yes, even as Moe was dictating his memoirs and Larry was sitting in the Old Actors Home, their moral descendants were drilling through walls and sneaking in windows. Behind it all sat Richard Nixon, a man of Moeish demeanor who, when asked point-blank who was responsible for the mess all around him, could stand up straight, look his questioner in the eye, pat his buddies on the back, and say, "They did it!"

16
The Effect of Curly on the Ford Administration

IF THE INFLUENCE *of the Stooges was most deeply felt during the Nixon presidency, that did not make Nixon the most Stoogely president. Rather, it was his successor, Gerry Ford (named after Jerry "Curly" Howard) who epitomized Stoogeliness in the Oval Office. Were Curly still alive, the role of President Gerry in a motion picture biography would be his for the asking.*

Act One, Scene One:

(Open on the office of the President of the United States. President Richard Nixon is meeting with his top advisor.)

NIXON: I tell ya, boys, those congressional committees are doin' an awful lot of snoopin' around. If they find out what we've been up to, it's Sing Sing for sure.

HALDEMAN: Yer right, boss. If only we had some chump to take the rap for us. Maybe we could give 'em Segretti.

(Erlichman, another aide, rushes in.)

ERLICHMAN: Bad news, boss! The feds just caught Spiro

93

taking bribes in the White House basement! He's goin' up the river!

NIXON: Oh no! My own vice president caught with his hands in the till! If I get my hands on that moron, I'll rip his esophagus out!

HALDEMAN: Whadda we do now, boss? With Spiro in stir, the feds are bound to come up here pokin' around.

ERLICHMAN: Not to mention, you've got to find a new vice president before the democrats plug you and put Tip O'Neil in!

NIXON: A new vice president, eh? A new vice president! Ha, Ha! Boys, I think our troubles are over.

HALDEMAN: What do you mean, boss?

NIXON: I think I've got the perfect sucker for the job—Curly Ford!

ERLICHMAN: Curly . . . but that mutton head can't walk and chew gum at the same time!

HALDEMAN: He hasn't got the brains of a Doberman pinscher.

ERLICHMAN: The Congress will know he can't be trusted with the country!

NIXON: Ha, ha, ha! Exactly!

HALDEMAN: Wait a minute, boss—you mean . . .

NIXON: Now you're catching on!

ERLICHMAN: Well, explain it to me.

HALDEMAN: With a bonehead like Ford in the vice presidency, they won't dare impeach the boss! No matter how bad we are, that knucklehead could only be worse!

ERLICHMAN: I get it! As long as Curly's number two, we'll always be number one! Boss, you're a genius!

NIXON: Ha, ha, ha. Ain't it the truth. *(To intercom:)* Rosemary, get Curly Ford on the line. Ha, ha, hahhh. Gentlemen, I think the future of our little operation is assured.

Scene Two:

(CURLY in White House basement, stepping over mops, pails.)

ERLICHMAN: And this is your office, Mister Vice President.

CURLY: What's that in the corner?

ERLICHMAN: Oh, that? It's a little "welcome aboard" gift from the president. A bucket of warm spit.

CURLY: Gee, that president's sure a swell fella. Say, Erly, where ya going?

ERLICHMAN: Uh, I've had a long day—I thought I'd go home and turn in.

CURLY: Oh, I get it—Erly to bed, Erly to rise! Nyuk nyuk nyuk. *(Erlichman exits. Moe and Larry enter.)*

MOE: Ya did it, kid! I can't believe it! Vice president and president pro tem!

CURLY: Yeah. Not only that, but I get to sit in at the Senate, too!

LARRY: And me as your press secretary!

MOE: And me as Secret Soivice!

ALL THREE: Secret Service day and night, we do the job and do it right! *(They laugh, light cigars.)*

LARRY: Ya know, this job is really somethin'. As vice president, you can do anything you want, and no one cares.

MOE: Unless somebody pops the prez, in which case you've got to take over the country.

CURLY: Ah, who'd ever shoot a great guy like the president?

LARRY: I don't know. Some of those Democrats are gettin' awful nasty with this Watergate business.

MOE: Say, you don't think any of those guys would try any funny stuff, do you?

LARRY: I don't know. Some of them are pretty mean.

CURLY: We gotta protect him! The president's my pal!

ALL THREE: Secret Service day and night, we do the job and do it right!

MOE: I got it! We'll make some tapes of the president without his knowin' it. That way we'll have proof that he's on the up and up!

LARRY: But how will we prove it to anybody else?

MOE: You're the press secretary! You'll leak the tapes to the press!

CURLY: Leak 'em?

MOE: Soitainly! We'll give Larry a code name. Those press guys don't believe anything you tell them straight out, but they believe *everything* anybody says on the Q.T.

CURLY: But how will we get the tapes?

MOE: As a Secret Service operative, I happen to know that the president already has a secret taping system set up by his plumbers!

CURLY: Plumbers! Why we're the finest plumbers who ever plumbed!

MOE: Exactly! We'll sneak into the Oval Office and grab the tapes. Then Porcupine here will feed them to the papers! The prez'll be cleared in no time.

Scene Three:

(Back in Curly's office a few days later.)

MOE: Did you give those tapes to that reporter?

LARRY: You bet! He called me Deep Throat!

MOE: Deep Throat? How come?

CURLY: Cause he blows so many gags! Nyuk nyuk nyuk. *(Moe tries to poke Curly's eyes. Curly blocks him.)*

RADIO: We interrupt this program to bring you an important bulletin! The president is a crook! The Congress today heard tapes of the president lying, cheating, and saying bad words. Faced with impeachment, the president has chosen to resign at once!

STOOGES: Nya ah ah!

MOE: Did you hear that? Kid, you're the new president! *(Curly swoons.)*

LARRY: Ah, he's fainted! *(Grabs bucket of warm spit and splashes Curly in the face.)*

MOE: Curly! Mister President! Say a few syllables!

CURLY: Mammmmmmmmmaaaaa!!

Act Two, Scene One:

(Curly in the Oval Office, going over legislative documents with Moe. Larry enters.)

LARRY: Mister President, the gentlemen of the press are waiting outside.

MOE: Let 'em wait!

CURLY: Yeah, we got pressing matters of state to attend to. *(Camera reveals Curly and Moe are playing tic-tac-toe.)*

MOE: I say, Jasper, what shall we do about the fall of Saigon?

CURLY: Poissonally, I prefer springtime in Saint Louie. *(Reporters rush in.)*

REPORTERS: Mister President! Mister President!

LARRY: Hold it down, hold it down. The president will recognize you all!

CURLY (to Moe): What's he talkin' about? I don't recognize any of 'em.

FIRST REPORTER: Mister President, how can you justify pardoning Nixon for all his crimes before he's even stood trial?

CURLY: When he was leavin' I came in to say goodbye and tripped and fell against him. He said, "Pardon me," and I said, "Soitainly."

SECOND REPORTER: What about the Democrats' move for a new minimum wage?

THIRD REPORTER: What about the new speed limit?

FOURTH REPORTER: And the oil embargo!

FIRST REPORTER: And the Mayaguez?

CURLY (to Moe and Larry): What do I say now?

MOE: Say you'll veto.

CURLY: I'll veto!

LARRY: He'll veto!

REPORTERS: He'll veto! *(Reporters rush out of room to phone in their stories.)*

CURLY: Say, this president stuff ain't so hard.

LARRY: Mister President, your itinerary calls for you to shoot golf with the Speaker of the House.

CURLY: Shoot golfs? I never even seen a golf! *(Moe knocks him on head.)* Oh, look at the golfs.

Scene Two:

(Stooges on golf course with Tip O'Neil and other dignitaries.)

CURLY (teeing up): Observe, gentlemen, a perfect birdy. *(Swings, looks around. Ball is lodged in Moe's eye. Curly does double take.)* Nya ah ah!

O'NEIL: Mister President, did you really tell reporters you didn't care if your daughter had affairs?

Second Dignitary: And that your son smokes marijuana!

Third Dignitary: And that your wife's an alcoholic!

Curly: Soitainly! Gotta make myself look good somehow.

O'Neil: But Mister President, what effect will these revelations have on affairs abroad?

Moe: Hey, don't get poissonal!

Second Dignitary: And wearing those short trousers to meet the Japanese minister!

Moe: His were just as short!

O'Neil: Mister President, these thoughtless actions are making you look bad!

Larry: Gowan, he's always looked like this. *(Suddenly Sarah Jane Moore bursts from the hedges brandishing a gun.)*

Moore: Die, President!

Curly: Hey, Moe! Hey, Larry!

Moe and Larry: Secret Service day and night, we do the job and do it right! *(Moe, Larry, and Curly leap on Moore in a pig pile. Cops arrive and take her away.)*

O'Neil: Mister President! You could have been killed!

Curly: Nya ah ah.

Moe: Nothing to it, gentlemen, nothing to it. No worse than that young scoundrel who ran into the president's car when we were taking a presidential shortcut through a red light! *(The party proceeds along the golf course. Suddenly Squeaky Fromm drops out of a tree, brandishing a pistol.*

Curly catches sight of the tassel on her elf's cap and goes wild, snorting and stomping like a bull.)

Second Dignitary: Look out, it's another one!

Moe: Never mind her! Watch out for him! Tassels make him crazy! *(Curly rams into Squeaky, who can't get her gun to fire. He butts her with his head, sending her flying into the water trap. Moe and Larry haul her out.)*

Moe: You'll get life for this, sister!

O'Neil: Mister President! What will you do now?

Curly *(calming down)*: Veto, veto, makes legislative bodies blue! I'll sign a million vetoes! Woowoowoowoowoo!

17
The Influence of the Three Stooges on the CIA

*T*HE FOLLOWING DOCUMENTS, *culled from almost four decades of Central Intelligence Agency correspondence, were obtained by the American Stooge Symposium just before President Reagan repealed the Freedom of Information Act.*

Top Secret, Eyes Only
From: Allen Dulles
To: John Foster Dulles
June 12, 1945

Dear Jack,

I guess you've heard the rumors about the war ending soon, and you know how nervous my boys at OSS are that they'll all lose their jobs. No doubt the Germans aren't going to provide us with much more of an excuse to play cloak and dagger around Europe, and from what I hear of the Manhattan Project's progress, the Orient is not going to be ripe much longer either. Can you think of any way to convince this new bird Truman that it's a good idea to keep a spy force together in peacetime? Better yet, can we convince him to let your

sweet brother run it? I know it's sort of un-American—
gentlemen reading other gentlemen's mail and all that—but
we've got ourselves a plush deal here with business
opportunities up the gazebo. FDR never would have stood for
it, but FDR's not here anymore, is he? What do you think?

Your Secret Sibling,

Al

July 2, 1945

To: President Harry S. Truman
From: Harry Hopkins

Dear Mr. President,

Regarding your query of July 1, under absolutely no
circumstances do I think it would be necessary, ethical, or
even legal to fund a full-time U.S. spy ring in peacetime.
Certainly President Roosevelt would not have considered any
such charter. Our enemies are conquered, and what sort of
example would we give the world if we were to repay our allies'
loyalty and sacrifice by spying upon them? These Dulles
brothers are bad news and Republicans to boot. Show them
the gate.

Loyally,

Harry Hopkins

To: A. Dulles
From: J. F. Dulles
July 9, 1945

Dear Al,

A little flak from the old guard, but I think our cat's in the

bag. I gave the president a copy of *A Tale of Two Cities*, but
he said it was full of "furriners." I tried *The Scarlet
Pimpernel*, but he didn't know what a pimpernel was.
Conrad's *The Secret Agent* put him to sleep, and when I tried
to explain about Mata Hari he pulled the shades and asked
me to repeat the dirty parts. Finally, with an ingenuity born of
despair, I hit upon a narrative the president could
understand. He at once saw the wisdom in establishing a
secret intelligence agency. I think you can go pick out your
trench coat.

Jack

To: Mrs. Harry S. Truman, Hannibal, Missouri
From: The White House
July 9, 1945

Dear Bess,

Gee willikers, what a time I'm having! Nobody ever told me
about this big bomb the fellas out West are working on! Hoo-
ee! They say it'll put a hole in Japan from column A to column
B! Haw-haw! I might even have them send one out to you to
get rid of them pesky gophers! That nice Mister Dulles who
sent you the box of chocolates came by the Oval Office today.
He looks to me to be about a 7 and ⅝ long oval, a mighty
smart man. Anyways, he says that I'm about the best
president he's known since U.S. Grant! Whadda ya think o'
them bananas? And he said he reckoned folks took to a nice
regular lady like yourself a lot more than they ever did to that
snooty-nosed Eleanor Roosevelt. Whoo, does that woman use a
lot of perfume! Riding in an elevator with her is like a hot day
at the funeral home. Anyhow, this Dulles fella tells me how
now that the war is over them Russians are gonna be
sneaking around America lookin' for our big bomb building
secrets. I said, "Well, Mister Dulles, I met Stalin, and I can tell
you he's an OK sort of Joe." Mister Dulles said that Stalin
might be jake but some of his assistants is tricky atheist

devils who'd like nothin' better than to use our big bomb on them poor little Chinamen. He says what we need is a secret spy force to beat the Ruskies at their own game! I said, "But, Mister Dulles, won't folks think it's a little unneighborly of us to start spyin'? I mean, we are kings of the ant heap now and we got this far without being sneaky." He says, "Well, sir, fact is if we didn't have spies down through history, there wouldn't be no America now at all! With that he pulled out some top-secret movin' pictures made during the Civil War, which clearly showed that back then the Union army had three gents named Larry, Moe, and Curly—"the very brains of the Secret Service"—who went behind Confederate lines to steal secrets. And were they ever wily! At one point this rebel general says to Moe, "The major can smell a spy a mile away!" Moe looks around and says, "Good thing he can't smell one any closer!"

That moving picture convinced me, and I even asked Mister Dulles if these three fellas might be available to head our new spy gang (he wants to call it the Central Intelligence Agency). Mister Dulles says, "No. After all, the Civil War was eighty years ago." But he said he and his brother could head up the new gang, just like these two fellas Moe and Curly (he looks a little like J. Edgar Hoover) were brothers. So now the U.S.A. has got a spy gang of its own, and we can be sure the Russians won't ever get a hold of our big bomb.

Love and xxx,

Harry

To: Congressman Richard Nixon
From: F. Dulles
11/14/49

Dear Dick,

I was watching the Stooges today and thinking about your problem with Hiss. It was the one where the boys are after some Jap spies and Curly gets his head caught in a jack-o'-lantern. Then it struck me. Look in the pumpkin patch!

You owe me one,

Mr. Dulles

From: CIA
To: The White House
February 24, 1962

Dear President Kennedy,

About this Castro problem: My boys think trick cigars might be just the thing. Seems the Stooges used them to great advantage when they were spies in *Uncivil Warriors*. If it worked for the brothers Howard, could it do less for the brothers Kennedy?

Blindly,

Wm. Casey

To: The President
From: National Security
April 28, 1970

Dear President Nixon,

Thank you for letting me have my way with Chile. Such faith in one's humble servants and select delegating of responsibility is the sign of a true statesman. Our operatives in that primitive land feel that once the junta has finished their coup, the best way to deal with the leftists is to herd them into Santiago Stadium and mow them down. Speaking of Moe, the idea for this comes from *Saved by the Belle*, in which the Three Stooges found themselves helping to suppress a revolution in a Latin American country. In the finale of this especially inspirational episode, the revolutionaries are all dragged off by "the people's friend"— the general who has grabbed power—to be executed in "the General Casino." Perhaps the Stooges thought such inspiration to be fantasy, but we have here the opportunity to imitate art. You didn't here this from me,

Henry

From: The White House
To: Henry Kissinger
February 3, 1980

Dear Doctor,

Thanks for sending over the clip of *Saved by the Belle*. Nancy and I laughed and laughed. Did I ever tell you about the time I stopped those three monkeys from getting residuals? Oh, I did. Oh. Anyway, I can see why you like that flick so much. But don't you think the earthquake-torn Latin country with the revolutionaries seizing power looks an awful lot like Nicaragua? Just to be on the safe side, I'm going to send a secret army down there to mine their harbors and harass their borders. Otherwise we're going to end like Curly— walking around with pillows tied to our behinds! Ha, Ha,

Ronald R.

From: The President
To: The Vice President
February 3, 1983

Dear George,

I don't care what your experience at CIA taught you, there's no reason we have to let the press come along every time we invade a foreign country. And no, D-Day *wasn't* as big a secret as my Grenada invasion. You want precedent. OK: in *Dutiful But Dumb*, the Three Stooges visited a country called

Vulgaria, which pulled off its illegal military operations by making it a law to shoot all photographers. Simple as that. So put that in your pipe and smoke it, mister. My invasion of Grenada was an exercise in the *Dutiful But Dumb* style.

Likewise I'm sure,

Mister President

18
The Influence of the Stooges on Feminism

PATRIARCHY! WHAT FORM of dictatorship has ever been so cruel or so unshakable? Imagine this scenario: You are a young woman, a virgin, in ancient Rome. You have all the dreams and desires, all the hunger for experience and independence young people share. Then, like a draft notice at the senior prom, comes an edict from the emperor: All red-headed maidens, eighteen to twenty-two years old, are to report to the emperor. You—the virgin—are chattel to the ruler. You—the woman—are slave to the man.

Thus begins *Matri Phony*, one of the Three Stooges' most devastating assaults on the subjugation of women by male oppressors. In order to protect a young maiden from this vile sexual conscription, Moe, Larry, and Curly not only defy the patriarchy, but cross a line few males of any generation dare navigate: they take on the oppressed woman's burden.

In order to give the young virgin time to escape, Moe dresses Curly as the bride and sends him into the emperor's bed chamber. "Go on," Moe tells his sacrificial cross-dresser, "get sexy!"

Not until *Black Like Me* did one of the insiders reach so far to comprehend the experience of the excluded. "Oh," the aroused emperor says of the veiled Curly, "a spirited wench!" This single scene opened a whole world of possibilities for the generation of young women who saw it. For the first time they understood that the restrictions they bore were not bound to their gender—that life's options were not cut off at the genitalia. When Curly took on the aspect of a woman and *resisted* the province of the aggressor, he inspired modern feminism, *Tootsie*, and the *Red Sonja* comic book.

But let us examine the stable into which the fertilizer of this possibility was deposited.

The history of the woman's movement in the twentieth century is the story of a slow, deliberate advancement in which each generation took two steps forward and was then pushed one step back. The turn-of-the-century suffragettes won the vote, but their progress was stopped by the onslaught of the Great Depression—a political catastrophe that forced families to fall back to traditional structure (the mother home with the hungry kiddies, Pop out pounding the pavement) and made sexual inequality seem an academic argument best reserved until families could again afford the luxury of debating.

The daughters of the suffragettes went off to the shipyards and assembly lines of World War II, proving that women could stand side by side with men in even traditionally masculine labors ("Moe, Larry, and Curly," said the first of three tall, strong babes, "meet Flo, Mary, and Shirley!"). When the GIs came home, flooding the job market, these second-generation feminists reluctantly hung up their welding masks and started breeding the baby boom.

But those boomers grew into a generation of women who would not be denied. When the children of the third generation reached adulthood, in 1970, they took up the volleyball their mothers and grandmothers had been forced to relinquish. In America in the 1970s, women refused to be girls any longer.

How were the ideals, the memories of dreams deferred, passed from one generation of women to the next? Not in books, for the men controlled the presses. Not at the family dinner table, for men dominated the shape of the conversation. Not in churches or in schools or on the field hockey court. No, the aspirations of the women's movement were carried,

Sensitive and yet still strong, the new man is born. Photo courtesy Columbia Pictures Corporation.

nurtured, and fanned by the Three Stooges. Curly, Larry, and Moe were the only male artists bold and visionary enough to see the validity of the agenda of the early suffragettes and not only adapt it to their own art but actually extend the modest goal of democratic representation to the greater dream of true equality. That they did their work unappreciated is not just evidence of Stoogely modesty; the revolutionary nature of their efforts made coding and iconography a necessity.

Now, though, the Stooges are gone, and women have come into their destiny. Time to pause and pay respect to those who led the way through the desert but never entered the promised land. Hail Moe, hail Curly, hail Larry! How far could feminism have gotten without these three men?

That is like asking how far Icarus could have ascended without his parachute.

Again and again, the Stooges donned women's guise to experience the world through women's eyes. In *Whoops, I'm an Indian*, Curly becomes the Indian bride of a French Canadian trapper. Pierre, filled with lust, leers at his reluctant conquest and exclaims, "Now I have for you ze beeg surprise!" How many women recognized in this hopeless boast the lame bravado of the aroused male, declaring himself expansive in the presence of irrefutable evidence to the contrary.

In *Micro-Phonies*, the Stooges befriend a talented female singer whose father (not all male oppression comes from husbands and lovers) has denied her a career in the arts. Curly again dons feminine raiment, lip-synchs to the daughter's voice, and—when the father expresses delight—reveals that it was his suppressed daughter the old man was applauding. Thus did Curly take on the form of a woman in order to expurgate the sins of men.

Do men humiliate women for their amusement? Well, then, the Stooges will dress as harem dancers (in *Wee Wee Monsieur*) that all men might, by identification, suffer such humiliation.

Perhaps Curly's most daring recognition of the envy men have for women came in *Mutts to You*. Charged with delivering a lost baby to its parents, Curly dressed himself as a mother. In doing so, he symbolically bore the baby, the great feat men are denied, and in vengeance for which they inflict so much pain on women. In assuming the role of childbearer, Curly acknowledged his womb-envy, and thus went far toward conquering it.

Do men treat women cavalierly? The Stooges held such actions up to ridicule. Listen to Curly's devastating mockery of such chauvinism: "I'll come home from a hard day's work, whistle for my dog, and my wife will come out. I'll have kids, dozens of them!"

Or recall this attack on the glamor industry that, in the words of famous wife Yoko Ono, "makes her paint her face and dance": in *Cookoo Cavaliers*, the Stooges find themselves with title to a Mexican beauty salon, and Moe cries, "There's a lot of money in making homely dames beautiful!"

The fool might hear this and call Moe himself a sexist, but the intent is clear: Moe seeks to show women who have made themselves ugly by accepting the yoke of patriarchy aware of their own inner beauty.

When a vile saloon owner brings to the Stooges his Latin dancing girls, seeking to have them bleached blonde to make them more alluring to men, Curly violently rejects this notion of the woman as sex-toy, even ripping out great chunks of the dancers' hair. No doubt they would thank him one day.

When, in their roles as census takers, the Stooges meet an older woman who—broken by the yoke of male expectations—insists she is twenty-nine years old, they grab her, force open her mouth, and count her teeth to ascertain her real age. Thus Moe and his feminist brothers forced liberation on those poor sex slaves too well indoctrinated to embrace it willingly. Lucky gal.

A great part of the Stooges' importance to feminism was in questioning the validity of marriage. The Stooges were the first to observe that marriage was a social contract designed to subjugate the woman, to make her a chunk of male property and tie her to the stove. ("Oh, darling," asks the oppressed bride in *Dutiful But Dumb*, "have you forgotten all your other wives?" "Completely," replies the wealthy rat Percival, "except on alimony day.") At a time when the institution was held sacred, Howard, Fine, and Howard declared it conscriptive sham and challenged the social order of their day, indeed of their whole culture. In the Stoogely oeuvre, women view marriage with canny detachment and an accountant's eye. The cruel male myth of romantic love does not fool these worldly dames.

The single women in *Oily to Bed, Oily to Rise* will marry the Stooges only if they save their farm (a farm run by women but threatened by corrupt men) and make them wealthy.

The women in *Brideless Groom* are appalled by Shemp as a prospective lover—until he becomes wealthy. No girl would want to marry Shemp, Moe explains, but a lot of girls would be interested in a million bucks. Shemp resists marriage even when a would-be bride clamps his head in a press and twists it slowly counterclockwise. Finally, womanhood wins, and Shemp is dragged screaming to his destiny.

Not that the Stooges portray women as materialistic; they

are simply savvy. The young maiden in *Men in Black* promises to marry the Stooge who does the most "for duty and humanity." These Stoogely women insist that they hold the purse strings in a buyer's market.

The women in *False Alarms* have no illusions about romantic love. One likes fireman Moe because he has a car. "Come on, girls!" she says to her sisters as soon as they have the Stooges in thrall. "Let's go places and eat things!" Males everywhere trembled in fear at this manifestation of the consuming female, the primordial archetype whose dreadful countenance fills the male subconscious with ancient anxiety and ties knots in his libido.

At one point Curly and the fat earth mother sit facing each other, exchanging face slaps in a scene that is at once a recognition of the male's attempted dominance and a celebration of the woman's ability to respond in kind to any show of force.

Kind of makes Germaine Greer look wimpy by comparison.

"Good morning, sir," says Moe the census taker in one short. "Are you married or happy?" A plate flies at the trembling man's head, and a female voice summons him back inside. "Married," concludes Moe, at once condemning the institution and acknowledging the solid pitching power pent up in that double X chromosome.

The ideal of a matriarchy is further explored in the ironically titled *Woman Haters* (the name, of course, a caustic comment on the male-supremacist attitude of the time). A lame, emasculated character named (symbolism steaming) "Mister Zero" declares, "I'll give you my opinion of the opposite sexes: when a man marries a girl he has to work while she relaxes." Mister Zero whines on about how the male is enslaved by the woman. Hardly the society of America in the 1930s! But a clear vision of the possibility the Stooges held up to young women whose notions of their sexual destinies were otherwise being formed by the male-supremacist fables of the day.

That film proceeds through an examination of the male characters' hypocrisy and moral turpitude, to a fascinating (and for 1934 risqué) denouement in which Moe and Curly tear Larry away from his bride on their wedding night. "Don't distoib us again," Moe orders the young wife. "We're going to bed!" Refusing to be thus abandoned, the bride charges into the Stooges boudoir to find the trio in bed together and entangled in what appears to be a spastic orgy. "Oh, a couple of acrobats!" she cries, hurling herself into bed with all three. "Move over!"

That it takes multiple partners to satisfy a woman was a concept introduced here and further explored (after the shocked silence of a generation's duration) by the great female philosophers Jong and Suzanne. The destruction of the male bonding is symbolized by what follows—the collapse of the marriage bed.

And English teachers think *Ethan Frome* is rich with symbolism!

The Three Stooges put an end to the era when a woman was yanked on a man's leash. No more would females be forced to define themselves by their husbands or remain as lost as the poor waif in *False Alarms*, who lamented, "The only way I can get a man to come see me is to call the doctor."

No, the Howards envisioned a society in which the man served the woman. A society in which, when Moe predicted, "We're gonna be paupers," Shemp replied, "Are you kiddin'? We're not even married."

19
The Effect of the Stooges on Madison Avenue

"THE BUSINESS OF America is business," declared one of our proud presidents just before the Depression came along and changed the business of the nation to social welfare. But while we may lose a generation to free-market incentives here and there, there's no question that for most of the demographic bulge this capitalistic system of ours has meant the security to go to sleep at night with a TV in every bookshelf and a TV dinner in every belly.

Yet the transformation from the old agricultural-based economy that preceded the Depression into our modern post industrial communications economy would not have been so smooth—indeed might never have taken place at all—without advertising. Yes, advertising—that great Western marriage of show biz, consumer service, psychology, avarice, and the sort of whopping tall tales that have framed American mythology from Paul Bunyan to Colonel Sanders. From the selling of Coca-Cola to the selling of the president, Madison Avenue has become the American Mecca, the holy land from which all power originates and toward which the mighty prostrate themselves.

And who was there on the frontier of the advertising age? Who designed the movement from snake oil sales to the self-definition of a culture? Who among you could have gotten this far in this book without guessing that in that mythical

Western manger where P. T. Barnum communes with the spirit of Henry Ford, the choirs of sales seraphim sing the names of Curly, Larry, and Moe?

The Stooges took the American taste for fast talk and fast money and made poetry of hyperbole. Whether selling Bright-O ("Bright-O, Bright-O, makes old bodies new/We'll sell a million bottles/Woowoowoowoowoo!") or "No Peddlers" signs, they convinced John Q. Public that he had a burning need for some product whose absence he'd never noticed. Supermarket checkout stands do a brisk business in books and pamphlets promising a wonder diet, how to flatten your stomach, how to get rid of love handles—all sold as impulse items right next to the candy bars. The fitness business has stayed big despite the untimely deaths of prominent jogging authors, Scarsdale diet doctors, and natural-food grazers. But who predicted the trend? Who was there before Jane Fonda ever lifted a leg? The Three Stooges, that's who. In *Spook Louder* (1942), the boys were marketing an electronic reducing machine, selling door to door and using Curly to demonstrate. When they sold one, Moe snapped into high Madison Avenue gear with a pre-science that would make the Green Giant proud. "Make out a receipt!" Moe barked at Larry when a customer put up his cash. "How do you spell *fifty*?" Larry asked. "Make it seventy-five," Moe whispered.

Peer pressure, too, was as useful a marketing tool for the Stooges as for the Pepsi Generation or designer jeans dealers. As Moe hawked greeting cards on the street in *Boobs in Arms*, those who didn't give in to his sales pitch were sneeringly dismissed with, "Oh, a snob, eh?" Like Madison Avenue after him, Moe implied that, if you were foolish enough to pass up whatever gimcrack he was peddling, you obviously had something wrong with you.

Think that the manufacturers of pet rocks and mood rings had good luck making people hungry for worthless objects? Well, they were pikers compared to Moe, who in *Heavenly Daze* sold investors on the idea of "a fountain pen that writes under whipped cream." It was almost as impressive as their famous "dog wash."

In *Termites of 1932* the Stooges were devoted to building a better mousetrap—one in which the mouse would catch his head in a tiny noose and hang. Grim as this sounds, fortunes are not made by the squeamish of stomach. Those whose gastrointestinal juices are easily upset would not have approved of the climax of *Goofs and Saddles*, in which Moe and the boys invent the machine gun by feeding cartridge belts into a meat grinder. They try out their invention, of course, on the local bad guys.

Madison Avenue made great strides once the Stooges gave it its blueprint. Mothers came to believe that they could win their children's love—and, most touching of all, their husband's praise and pride—by buying Twinkies, using spray starch, and filling the toilet with blue liquid. Horny young gentlemen were told that they'd win the prom queen's heart by rinsing their mouths with Listerine, while lonely girls were promised romance in exchange for scraping the outer enamel off their teeth. If these were lies, they were harmless lies, for many young men did find their courage when bolstered by antiseptic breath, and many dentists prospered from smiles abraded by tubes of sex appeal.

The Mad. Ave. dictum—the seduction of insecurity by opportunity—was perhaps best voiced by Moe in *Micro-Phonies*: "Use Gritto, radio fans, to give your hands that dishpan look! How will your old man know you're working if you don't have dishpan hands?"

Frank Perdue was never more articulate, Lee Iacocca no more convincing.

APPENDIX: STOOGOLOGICAL GUEST LECTURES

I. The Development of the Three Stooges' Spiritual Thought

MOE, LARRY, AND Curly had a great influence on the evolution of religious thought in the twentieth century: from (a) unthinking piety to (b) "God is dead" nihilism to (c) the current rebirth of an Americanized—some would say bastardized—fundamentalism. The lantern of theology held high, the Stooges blazed the winding path so many thinkers of our time were to follow later.

The religious impulse was often disguised in the work of Curly, Larry, and Moe, probably in deference to the general sensitivity of the subject in the era in which they worked. Yet the Stoogely Trinity dealt with religious themes with both subtlety and a vigorous intelligence, eventually influencing and redirecting much of the theology of our age.

Although the Stooges were of the House of David, Jewish orthodoxy is scarcely glimpsed in their work. It is probably fair to say that the Stooges had their roots in Judaism but used the Hebrew faith only as a foundation for molding a fresh theology, much in the manner of the early Christians, Moslems, B'hai, and Rastafarians.

At times the Stooges made allusions to paganism, the ancient myths of the Greeks and Romans. In *An Ache in Every Stake*, Curly was forced to drag a huge ice block up a great hill over and over again. Each time he reached the summit the ice would melt and he would have to begin again. In *Back to the*

Woods, Larry is bound to a tree, where a great bird descends to peck at him.

These classical references should not be taken as evidence of a Stoogely belief in the gods of Olympus; rather, they seem to be an acknowledgment of that Western religious heritage from which Curly, Larry, and Moe's own theology grew.

The trio were also knowledgeable about pantheism and animism, as they demonstrated in the sort of scenes where they would frighten Arabs and Negroes by forming a human totem pole and claiming to be an evil sprit.

Christianity seems to have held little relevance for Moe, whose world view clung closer to the Old Testament "eye for an eye" than to the Christian "turn the other cheek." Moe reacted quickly to any provocation (much like the citizens of present-day Israel) with eye pokes and head knocks. Larry and Curly, however, fluctuated between Old Testament retaliation and New Testament acceptance and cheek-offering. As with many contemporary Christians, their theology of retribution was usually influenced by whether the person doing the slapping was stronger or weaker than they. If it was Moe, resistance was usually deferred.

In the thirties and forties, Howard, Fine, and Howard seemed to be disinclined toward any traditional religion at all. In *Disorder in the Court*, Curly takes the oath several times, each time omitting "so help me God." If that subtle snub was missed by the larger audience, it certainly was picked up by Sartre, Camus, and other philosophers who began questioning the role of the Deity only after Moe, Larry, and Curly paved the way. (While this is not a discussion of the French existentialists, the serious student of philosophy must also recognize that Curly's running joke, "I can't tell if it's half empty or half full," was picked up by lesser philosophers who found in this minor Stoogely nugget enough food for thought to round out curriculums and make into wall posters.)

The Stooges' own view of Christianity was perhaps best illustrated in *Malice in the Palace*, in which a robed man rides into a Middle Eastern city on an ass, palm leaves swaying before him. The Stooges follow immediately after, riding in a sleigh and all dressed as Santa Claus. Was the secularization and commercialization of the Christian religion ever commented on with more deftness, with fiercer wit? If Bertrand Russell had had any sense of shame, he'd have tossed in the towel right then and there.

With the death of Curly, though, the surviving Stooges seem to have been inclined toward deeper reflection on the nature of immortality. This new penchant for a traditional spiritual impulse was first revealed in *Heavenly Daze*, in which Shemp (himself bound to cross the Jordan not long after) arrives in Heaven to face a God who looks a lot like Moe ("The Lord," scripture assures us, "made man in his own image." "In that case," responds the wag, "he is not to be congratulated.") The Deity informs Shemp that he's destined for hell ("Bring the asbestos suit"), apparently for sins of the flesh (Shemp's wings become erect when a cute angel babe passes by).

It is clear that Shemp is, at this point, in neither heaven nor hell, though he seems to have been wherever he is for long enough to get acclimated. It is often assumed that Shemp is portrayed as being in purgatory, though since he was never baptized, some theologians may place him in limbo. This is a question of some complexity, as the presence of the Divine Countenance seems to rule out the limbo option, even as the strong likelihood of impending damnation appears to preclude this being purgatory (from which one can only go up). In this, too, the Stooges broke with orthodoxy to suggest a personal judgment before Armageddon.

Shemp is given one opportunity to redeem his soul: he must cure the surviving Moe and Larry of their sinful ways. Here is demonstrated a further tenet of Stoogely theology: that redemption and damnation are attained not through grace, as most Protestant churches maintain, but through works. Either that, or God just likes to make tainted souls jump through hoops.

The sinful nature of sex is reinforced when angel Shemp whistles at an attractive woman and gets a lightning bolt in the ass.

The theology of the Stooges is almost Calvinistic in its harshness. It offers a world where life is full of knuckleheads, and death only makes things worse. It is not surprising that, of the world's great religions, it was Catholicism that was most influenced by this Stoogely vision. (See *Last of the Moe Haircuts*, "The Influence of the Three Stooges on the Modern Papacy.")

II. Moe as Older Brother

*A*T THIS POINT *in our text, it may be worthwhile for readers to reflect on what they have learned thus far about the influence of the Stooges' characters on their art and their art on our culture. To that end, we offer here an essay by the great psychohistorian Mighty Joe Jung on the filial relationships among the Three Stooges themselves.*

One of the most common misconceptions about the Three Stooges is that Moe had a bad temper. Nothing could be further from the truth. Like most oldest children, Moe was as sweet-tempered as a mother goose, in spite of the idiotic and constant provocations of his younger siblings. The student who examines all the evidence with an unprejudiced eye will discover that, far from crabby or short-fused, Moe was in fact the living embodiment of patience. In this he exhibited a trait quite common to oldest children.

It's a well-documented fact that firstborns constitute 90 percent of all persons who lead creative, successful, or artistically productive lives. The few recognized cases of later siblings who succeed at anything noteworthy or worthwhile are generally credited to extraordinary circumstances forcing the younger sibling to imitate and take over for an incapacitated older brother or sister. Thus the death of Joe Kennedy, Jr., led to the assumption of responsibility and ambition by JFK, whose death led to Bobby's ascension, whose death led to Teddy's becoming torchbearer. In the same way, Sonny Corleone's assassination led to the rise of the wimpy brother who had to be killed by Michael for him to become godfather. Perhaps this myth is best embodied in American culture (the

Russians have their Karamazovs) by the Cartwrights: Adam's leaving the Ponderosa led to Hoss assuming the oldest-brother mantle and authority; when Hoss died, Little Joe was finally allowed, at age forty-two, to stop being called "little."

Moe, of course, never relinquished his *primo geniture* from the moment Shemp left the Stooges' act in prehistoric times. But the attempts by Larry and Curly to push him aside made the efforts of Michael Corleone look like valentines.

Let's look at *Cash and Carry.* Now a casual observer (prejudiced by the whinings of younger siblings we are all exposed to throughout our lives) might say, "Oh, that Moe is so mean to poor Larry and Curly! The big bully should leave them alone!"

But what does scientific examination show us? That Moe endures grief after grief from the other two idiots before finally running out of cheeks to turn and establishing a little necessary discipline: Moe makes no response when Curly and Larry drop their tools on his foot, drop a thick plank of wood on his neck, grind his head—already lodged in a hole in one wall—into the opposing wall, pull the floor out from under him, hurl him into a pit, drop a bucket on his head, and strike him repeatedly in the eye, head, and abdomen with picks and shovels. Finally, after all that, Moe is abused enough to poke Larry in the eyes and slap Curly's cheek. Well, who wouldn't? Far from the bully that the whining younger siblings allege him to be, Moe is the soul of restraint and forgiveness. Again and again, his moronic younger siblings abuse and injure him; again and again he restrains righteous retaliation. When self-preservation finally demands some minimal response, the guardians of the stupidly dangerous decry that defense as aggression.

Kind of like the UN.

Moe is the most unjustly maligned of older brothers. But all oldest children know the grief he endures. How many times has every oldest kid come home from a hard day at second grade only to find the baby has smashed his model airplanes, defecated on his comic books, and used his forty-fives as skateboards? And when the concerned older kid instructs the younger in the social disadvantages of such behavior (often using the only reinforcement younger kids comprehend—physical discipline) for the younger's own sake, how do mothers and other authority figures respond? By whacking the already abused older sibling and calling him a bully!

Meanwhile, the guilty younger one wails and cries for mother's sympathy while giving the broken model airplane another little kick.

Was Moe being mean in *Dizzy Pilots* when he slapped Curly? Yes? Well let's look at what Curly and Larry did to Moe before he responded. They caught his hand in a vise, they dropped him in liquid rubber, they inflated the rubber and let him float away, they poked him—airborne—in the head with a long pole, and then they deflated him by shooting him with a rifle. Still, *Moe made no retaliation*. Finally, when Curly tried to saw Moe's arm off, he responded with a little love tap. That's not short temper; that's self-preservation.

Sometimes Moe's oldest-sibling rage even extended to the animal kingdom. In *Whoops, I'm an Indian*, he goes fishing. Every time he hauls up a little fish, he tells it, "Go get your big brother!" and tosses it back in. Is this a highly developed sense of fairness or just a soft heart? Most firstborn children have both.

Moe took the burden of all oldest kids on his own shoulders—and for this all members of this noble but abused minority owe him allegiance. It's the older brothers, after all, who end up in the White House, while the younger ones usually gravitate toward penal colonies and fat farms. Family tragedy? Yes, but one as old as Cain and Abel. How much grief could be spared each generation if parents would only step aside and let all oldest siblings dispense a little Moe-ish discipline?

III. Moe's Greatest Threats

"I'm going to pull your tonsils out and stick 'em right in your eye!"

"I'll mash your head like a potato!"

"I'll knock your teeth out!"

"I'll make powder out of you!"

"I'll crack your head open!"

"I'm going to baste you in nitric acid!"

"I'll gouge your eyes out!"

"I'll bat your ears down!"

"I'll bite you!"

"If you so much as breathe, I'll tear your tonsils out and tie 'em around your neck for a bow tie!"

"I'll squeeze the cider out of your Adam's apple!"

"I'll knock your head right through your socks!"

"I'll annihilate you!"

"I'll exterminate you!"

"Say yes now or I'll strangle you!"

"Go to sleep or I'll murder you!"

"Get out of this house before I split your head open from ear to ear!"

"Mingle or I'll mangle!"

"Blow out the candles or I'll blow out your brain!"